The Genius of the Royal Academy

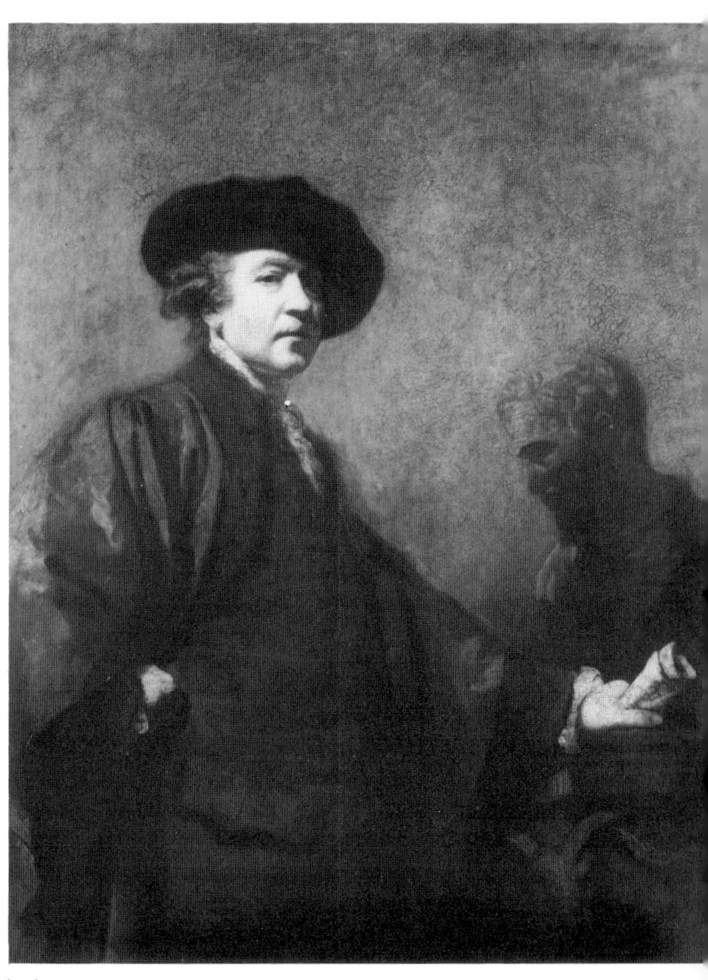

Frontispiece
SIR JOSHUA REYNOLDS, P.R.A.
Self-Portrait as D.C.L., c. 1773–80
oil on canvas, 127 × 101cm.(50 × 40in.)
Royal Academy of Arts, London
Reynolds received his Honorary Doctorate of Civil Law from Oxford University in 1773.

The Genius of the Royal Academy

Eric Shanes

The Royal Academy
John Murray

For
Joyce

Designed and produced by The Mallord Press
7 Cumberland Road, London W3

Printed by Raven Oak Press Ltd.,
40 Leythe Road, London W3 8AW

ISBN 0 7195 3919 6

TK INV

It will be no small addition to the glory which this nation has already acquired from having given birth to eminent men in every part of science, if it should be enabled to produce, in consequence of this institution, a School of English Artists. The estimation in which we stand in respect to our neighbours, will be in proportion to the degree in which we excel or are inferior to them in the acquisition of intellectual excellence, of which Trade and its consequential riches must be acknowledged to give the means ; but a people whose whole attention is absorbed in those means, and who forget the end, can aspire but little above the rank of a barbarous nation.

Sir Joshua Reynolds
Discourse IX
16 October, 1780

The Royal Academy of Arts in London

> We...beg leave to inform your Majesty, that the two principal objects we have in view are, the establishing a well-regulated School or Academy of Design, for the use of students in the Arts, and an Annual Exhibition, open to all artists of distinguished merit, where they may offer their performances to public inspection and acquire that degree of reputation and encouragement which they shall be deemed to deserve.

The Memorial containing these words was signed by twenty-two artists and submitted to King George III on 28 November, 1768. It stated the aims of the proposed Royal Academy of Arts and sought permission for the foundation of the institution. The King's response was favourable, and accordingly, the 'Royal Academy of Arts in London, for the purpose of cultivating and improving the Arts of Painting, Sculpture and Architecture' came into existence soon afterwards.

By acting as a forum for the cultivation of the fine arts the Royal Academy assisted their growth through the following century, a period of excellence in British art that has never been equalled. Reynolds, Wilson, Fuseli, De Loutherbourg, Turner, Constable, Lawrence and many other painters form a body of artists of international stature. Together they constitute the genius of the Royal Academy.

A Royal academy was sorely needed in 1768. Art education, the first of the two aims stated above, scarcely existed. There were academies of art in France and Italy but their educational value was very limited and they were virtually inaccessible. In the seventeenth century there had been two academies in London but neither of them were devoted exclusively to the fine arts. Probably the first such institution in Britain was created by a group of artists in 1711 in Great Queen Street. It was actively supported by Sir Godfrey Kneller, then the leading British portrait-painter. However, this institution soon disappeared after disagreement about its administration. It was followed by a similar school in 1720 which was founded by the history painter James Thornhill. It occupied premises in St. Martin's Lane and included Hogarth amongst its pupils. Hogarth later married Thornhill's daughter and after his father-in-law's death in 1734 he moved the academy to Peter Court, St. Martin's Lane where it survived for another thirty or so years. Apart from these impermanent foundations, however, there was no regular institutional instruction in the disciplines of drawing, painting and sculpture in Britain until the appearance of the Royal Academy Schools.

Another problem that faced artists was the attitude of collectors towards contemporary art. Then, as now, these purchasers preferred the familiar to the new and unusual. Furthermore, the largely aristocratic clientele for works of art favoured the work of Continental artists. This was, perhaps, more a measure of the prevailing fashion than an indication of real interests, but it aroused Hogarth's ire in particular. He clearly felt that the English preferred a second-rate Continental to a first-rate English picture:

> Paintings are considered as pieces of furniture; and Europe is already over-stocked with the works of other ages. These, with copies countless as the sands on the sea-shore, are bartered to and fro, and are quite sufficient for the demands of the curious, who naturally prefer scarce, expensive, and far-fetched productions, to those which they might have on low terms at home. Who can be expected to give forty guineas for a modern landscape, though in ever so superior a style, when he can purchase one which, for little more than double the sum, shall be sanctioned by a sounding name, and warranted original by a solemn-faced connoisseur?

The taste for Continental Old Masters, however, was not a problem entirely of the public's choosing. Contemporary British works were rarely exhibited prior to 1768, and there were to be no public art galleries in Britain until 1814. Virtually the only way for artists and connoisseurs to see the works of contemporary artists, and often even the Old Masters, was either by means of engravings, or occasionally at auctions. Otherwise it was a matter of gaining admittance to Royal or private collections or of embarking on the expensive and arduous Grand Tour. The Royal Academy was to have a remarkable effect in ameliorating this cultural destitution.

The origins of the institution lay in the collection of contemporary works of art given to the Foundling Hospital, an orphanage founded by Captain Thomas Coram that was awarded a Royal Charter in 1739. This collection was started by Hogarth who had donated his full-length portrait of Captain Coram to the Foundation in 1740 (Ill. 1). Other artists followed his example and eventually the collection included works by Reynolds, West, Gainsborough and Wilson, among others. Visits to see this important group of pictures became a fashionable court activity (the hospital was an extremely popular charity) and in 1746 the artists, led by Hogarth, decided to meet annually to decide how they might help the hospital. The resultant dinners grew in size and finally included over 150 artists. At one such feast in 1759 they resolved to meet further to consider proposals for an exhibition of contemporary art. These plans materialised in an exhibition in the following year at the premises of the Society of Arts in the Strand. This was a great success and attracted over 12,000 visitors. In 1761 a group of artists repeated the success in an exhibition held in Spring Gardens, Charing Cross (for which purpose they formed 'The Society of Artists in Great Britain'). The show included works by Hogarth and Reynolds and the first painting publicly exhibited by Gainsborough. Hogarth made designs for the covers of the catalogue and used the tail-piece to satirise the taste of the nobility for works by deceased Continental artists. The Society of Artists continued to exhibit annually and in 1765 obtained a Royal charter as 'The Incorporated Society of Artists in Great Britain'. It had more than two hundred members and continued to hold successful exhibitions although the viewing conditions were not ideal. A visitor to the 1762 exhibition tells of 'a sweating room, choked with clouds of dust'. Although the dust gave the paintings a dull appearance, one of the members, Richard Wilson, also cared little for the pallid qualities of the pictures themselves. In 1763 he and Benjamin

West were responsible for hanging the works and they attempted to counter their deficencies by resorting to a rather drastic measure:

> When the pictures were all up Wilson began to rub his eyes as if to clear them of something painful. 'I'll tell you what, West', he said, 'this will never do. We shall lose the little credit we have, for the public will never stand such a shower of chalk and brickdust'. 'Well', said West, 'but what is to be done? We can't reject their pictures now'. 'No, but we can mend their manners'. 'What do you mean?' 'You shall see,' said Wilson, 'what Indian ink and Spanish liquorice can do.' He accordingly despatched the porter to the colourman and druggist for these *reformers*, and dissolving them in water actually washed nearly half the pictures in the exhibition with this original glaze. 'There!' he said, 'it's as good as asphaltum, with this advantage that if the artists don't like it they can wash it off when they get the pictures home.'

By 1767, however, the Incorporated Society was riven with quarrels over the hanging of pictures and it disintegrated in the autumn of 1768. The architect William Chambers (Ill. 2) thereupon took a decisive step. He had been one of George III's tutors when Prince of Wales, and enjoyed easy access to the King. As the first minutes of the Royal Academy tell us:

> Some time towards the latter end of November, 1768, Mr. Chambers waited upon the King and informed him that many artists of reputation, together with himself, were very desirous of establishing a Society that should more effectually promote the arts of design than any other yet established, but they were sensible that their design could not be carried into execution without his Majesty's patronage...

The King was receptive to Chambers' approach and on 28 November he received a deputation that included Chambers, G.M. Moser (a painter and the King's drawing-master), Frances Cotes and Benjamin West. They submitted the Memorial quoted

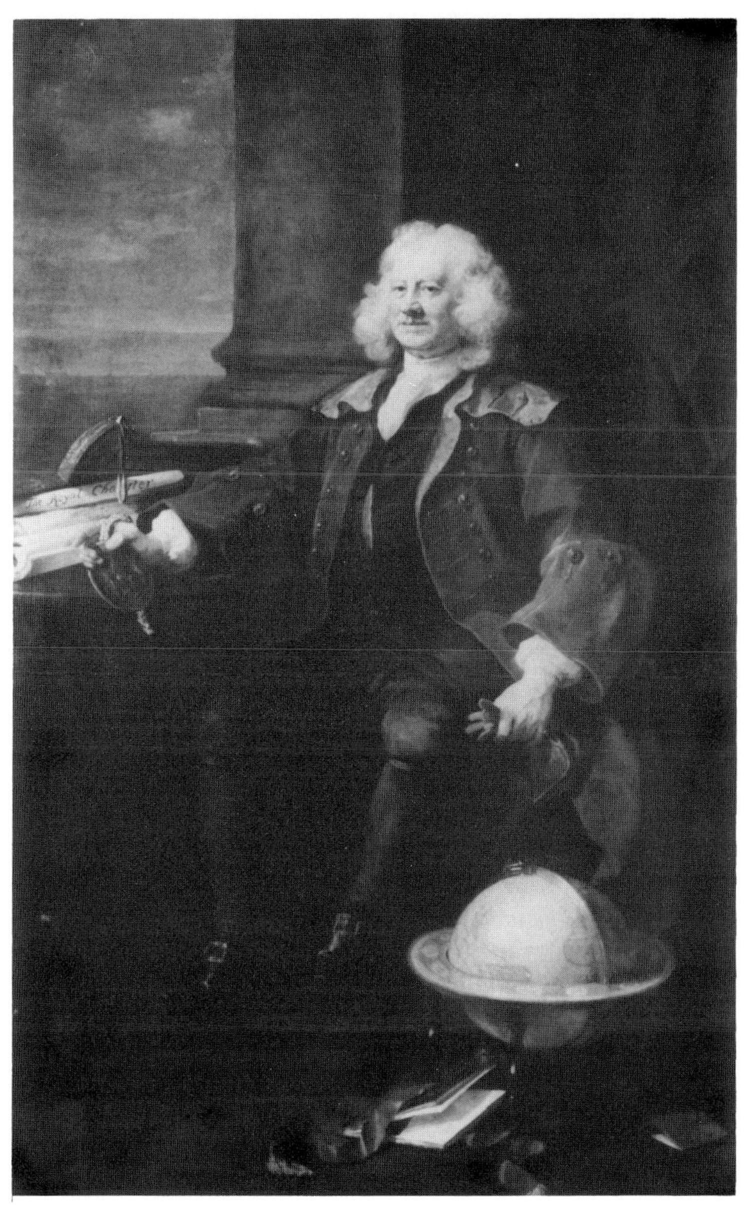

1
WILLIAM HOGARTH
aptain Thomas Coram of the Foundling Hospital, 1740
oil on canvas, 238 × 147cm.(94 × 58in.)
Thomas Coram Foundation for children, London
ı the table at the left is the Royal Charter of the undling Hospital; the globe alludes to the Captain's val career. Hogarth had offered this picture as the prize a raffle on behalf of the hospital, to which he gave the sold tickets; one of them held the winning number.

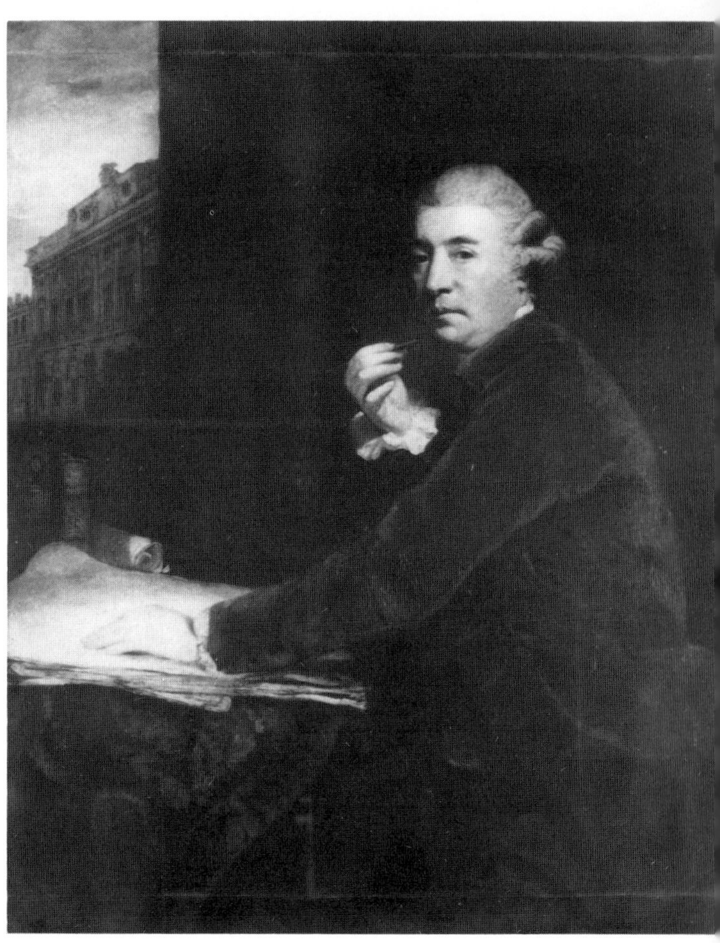

2
SIR JOSHUA REYNOLDS, P.R.A.
Sir William Chambers, 1780
oil on canvas, 127 × 101cm.(50 × 40in)
Royal Academy of Arts, London
Somerset House, which Chambers re-designed, can be seen on the left.

above and the King received it favourably. He requested written plans for the institution and Chambers accordingly lost no time in drawing up a detailed outline. This plan, known as the 'Instrument of Foundation of the Royal Academy', was the document by which the institution formally came into existence. It was placed before the King on 7 December, and signed by him on Saturday, 10 December, 1768.

The idea of a 'Royal' academy of arts appealed to the monarch who was a cultivated man, having studied the arts. Under Chambers' tutelage he had produced a great number of excellent architectural elevations, and after his accession in 1760 he was rumoured to have exhibited two landscapes at the Society of Artists. Eventually, this direct royal patronage would sometimes lead to disagreements, especially when the Academy asserted its independence. At first, however, the King agreed not only to recognise the institution, but also to make up any financial deficit it incurred out of the Privy purse. This he did for the first few years of the Academy's existence, after which it began to pay its own way and it has done so ever since.

The Instrument of Foundation defined the rules for election of members, set out the procedures for the appointment of the necessary Professors and lesser officers, and in general declared the manner and methods by which the organisation should be run. It also established the regulations of the annual Exhibition and the Schools. Forty Academicians were to be elected from among the contributors to the exhibitions, and an essential condition of election was to be the deposit of a Diploma Work such as a painting, bas-relief or other specimen of ability. Engravers were initially excluded from eligibility as Academicians, but soon afterwards the rules were amended to include them as Associates (in 1853 they became eligible for election as Academicians). In addition, the whole class of Associates was expanded in number to twenty members and election as an Associate became a necessary prelude for elevation to the upper body. Since 1971 the Membership of the Royal Academy has consisted of fifty Royal Academicians and twenty-five Associates, composed of painters, sculptors, engravers and architects. The pictures for the Summer Exhibition are chosen by an annually-rotated selection committee. Until 1903 both Academicians and non-members could submit up to eight works for exhibition (the works of Academicians having automatic right of display in the category of their election) but since then, due to demands for space, Academicians are allowed six works and non-members three.

An annually-appointed governing council, originally comprising the President and eight members, was appointed to supervise the day-to-day running of the Academy. This council served, and still serves, for two years, but each year half of its

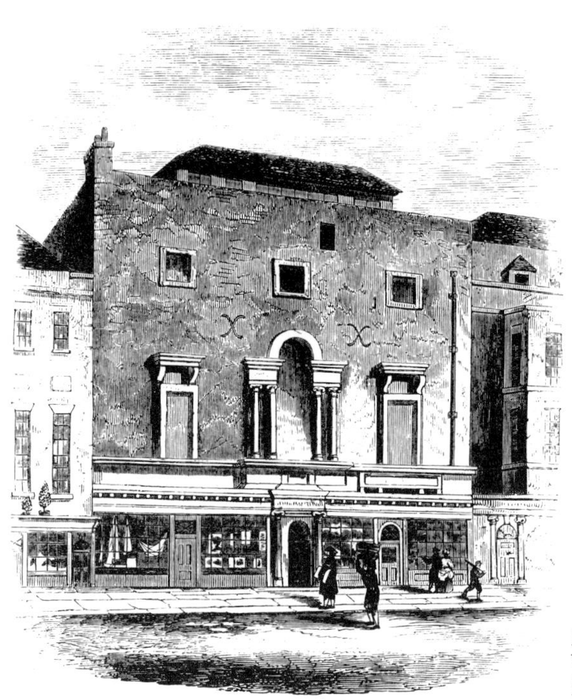

3
View of the Royal Academy in Pall Mall (engraving).

members retire so as to ensure an annual change in its composition. After some hesitation Joshua Reynolds agreed to be the first President of the Royal Academy. He was unanimously elected and knighted not long afterwards. Characteristically, for he did not care much for the company of his fellow painters, he had his friends Doctor Johnson and Oliver Goldsmith appointed to the posts of Academy Professors of Ancient Literature and History respectively; later holders of the latter office included Gibbon and Gladstone. Chairs of Painting, Architecture, Perspective and Anatomy were also created. The schools were supervised by nine annually-elected Visitors and by 1769 seventy-seven students, for whom the tuition was free, were enrolled. These included Joseph Farington, John Flaxman and Thomas Banks. By the turn of the century they had been followed by, among others, John Soane, Thomas Malton, William Blake, Thomas Lawrence, Joseph Mallord William Turner, Benjamin Robert Haydon, David Wilkie and Augustus Wall Callcott. Some famous later students included William Holman Hunt, Dante Gabriel Rossetti, John Everett Millais, Edward Lear, Arthur Hughes and Norman Shaw, the architect. Gold and silver medals

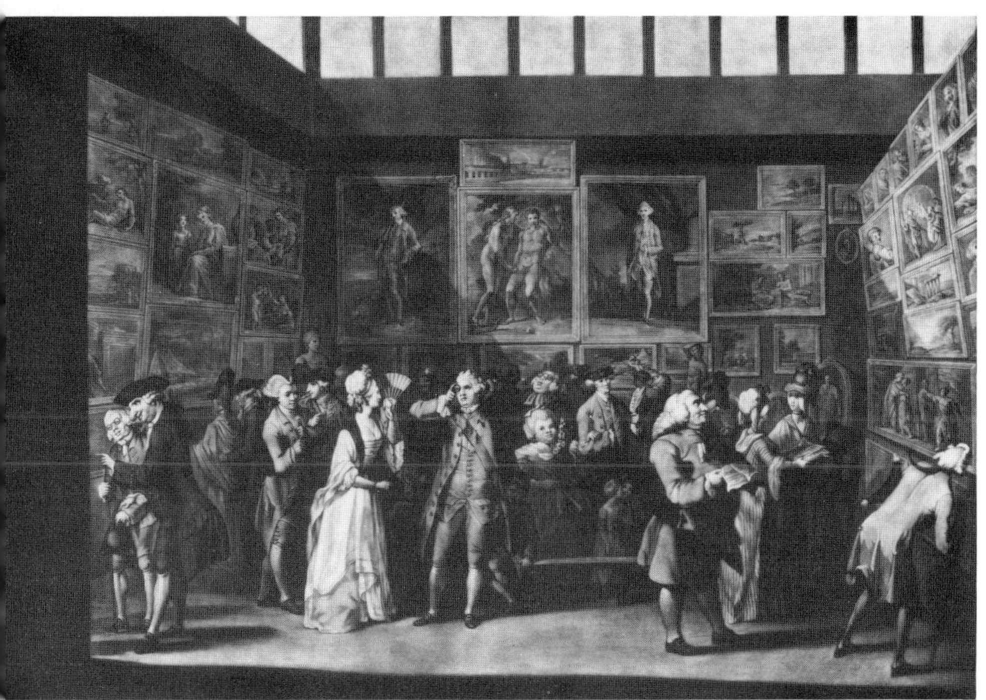

4
Richard Earlom after CHARLES BRANDOIN
The Exhibition of the Royal Academy, 1771
mezzotint engraving.

were instituted from the outset to encourage the students, and from 1768 Academicians were issued with a Diploma signed by the Sovereign upon their appointment. Annual dinners for the members and their guests have been held since the 1770s.

Reynolds set the intellectual and artistic standards of the Academy from the beginning. Between 1769 and 1790 he delivered fifteen eloquent Discourses in which he discussed the nature and practise of art, explored the qualities of artists such as Raphael, Michelangelo and Gainsborough, and stated the intellectual and formal requirements of late eighteenth-century art, qualities he characterised as the Great Style. Reynolds was succeeded as President by Benjamin West in 1793 and later Presidents have included Sir Thomas Lawrence, Lord Leighton, Sir John Everett Millais, Sir Edward Poynter and Sir Edwin Lutyens.

The first of the annual Exhibitions was held in 1769. It was the smallest of all the successive summer shows, with only 136 works on display. Ten years later this number had grown to more than 400, although that figure still seems slight when compared with the average of some 1400 that now fill the vast spaces of Burlington House every year. Then, however, the exhibition space was more limited. Between 1769 and 1779 the annual Exhibitions were held in premises on the south side of Pall Mall in a building that had been used previously as a print-warehouse (Ills. 3 and 4), although in 1771 the Academy's administrative offices and schools were removed to much more salubrious premises, some State apartments in Old Somerset House (Ill. 5) which were made available by the King. The Exhibition was held

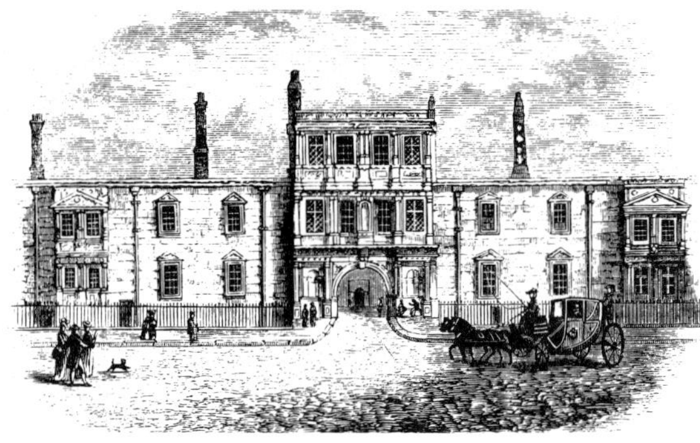

5
Part of Old Somerset House occupied by the Royal Academy (engraving).

there after 1780 when William Chambers' rebuilding of Inigo Jones' original structure was almost complete. It was envisaged that Somerset House would be the home of various learned societies and several government departments, and the Academy's annual Exhibitions were assigned to the Fine Rooms, a specially designed suite of rooms in the northern Strand block (Ill.6). The principal space in the block was taken up by the Great Room on the top storey where the largest and most important works were displayed (Ills. 7 and 8). At the time the Great Room was the largest public exhibition space in Britain, measuring fifty-three feet long by forty-three wide. Lesser rooms contained the antique Academy, the Library, the Assembly (or lecture) room and the Life Schools. The various levels were joined by a superb staircase (Ills. 9 and 10) which not only gave access to the public, but up and down which the works themselves were transported. The staircase presented problems to some visitors, especially the

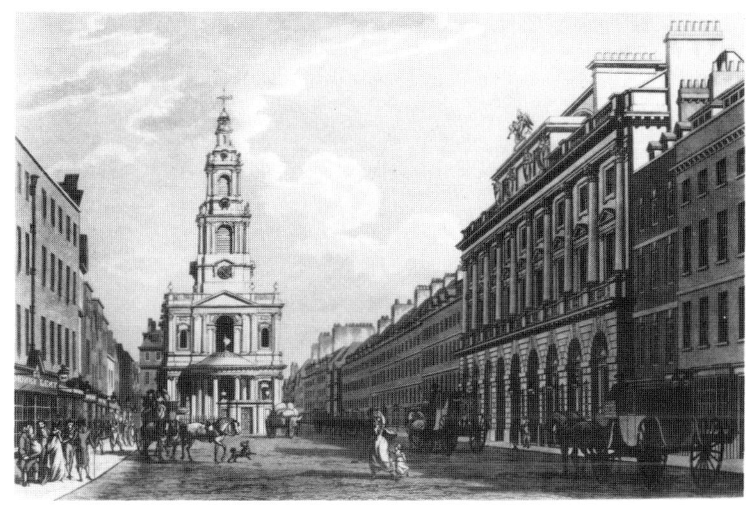

6
THOMAS MALTON
Somerset House in the Strand, aquatint
e Royal Academy occupied the block on the right.

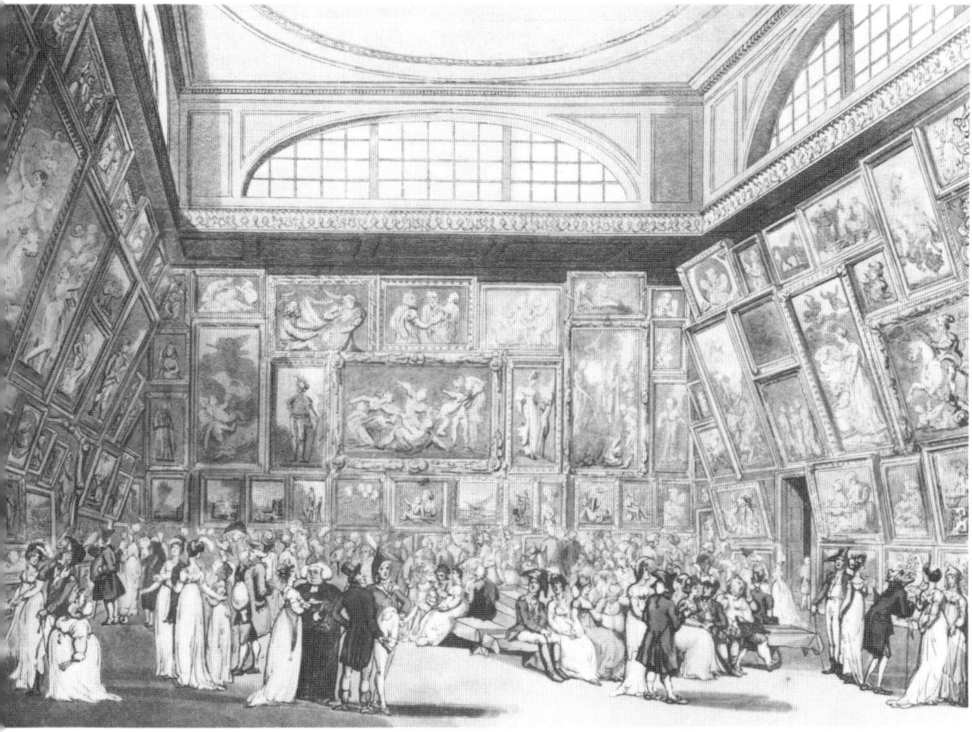

7
after THOMAS ROWLANDSON
he Exhibition Room, Somerset House, 1808, aquatint

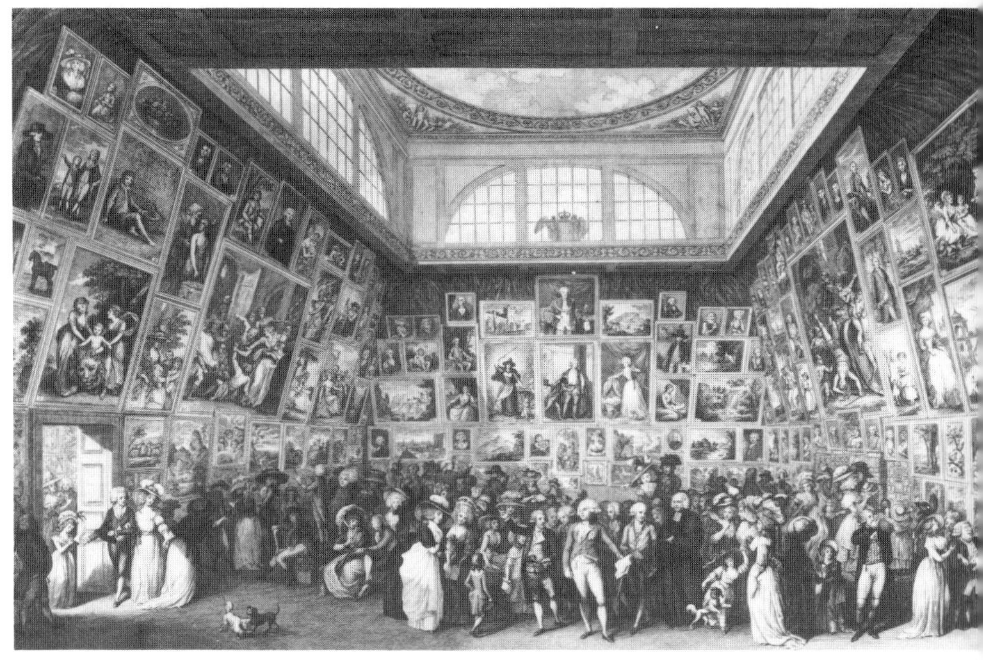

8
Pietro Martini after J.H. RAMBERG
The Exhibition of the Royal Academy, 1787, engraving
In the centre of the Great Room the Prince of Wales is being escorted by Sir Joshua Reynolds (holding his ear trumpet). Note the admittance of dogs to the exhibitions. The 'line' is clearly visible at the height of the top of the door. The motto *Let no stranger to the Muses enter* was inscribed in Greek above the doorway outside.

elderly or overfed. Queen Charlotte had to recuperate on each floor before ascending further and Doctor Johnson regarded the climb as a major test of endurance.

Academicians, of course, enjoyed an automatic right to exhibit without having to submit to the selection committee. Occasionally mix-ups occurred with embarrassing results:

> ... a small landscape was brought to judgement; it was not received with favour. The first judge said, 'That's a poor thing'; the next muttered 'It's very green'; in short, the picture had to stand the fire of animadversion from everybody but Constable, the last remark being 'It's devilish bad – cross it' [i.e.

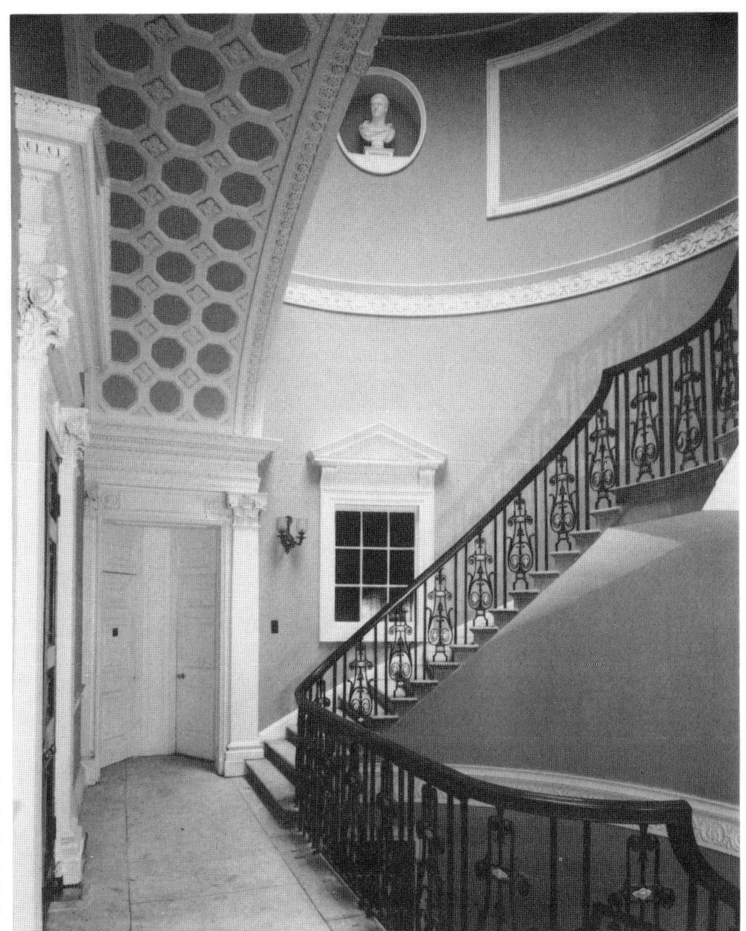

9
The staircase and first-
›or landing at Somerset
House (photograph,
courtesy of the
Department of the
Environment).

reject it]. Constable rose, took a couple of steps in front, turned around and faced the Council. 'That picture', he said, 'was painted by me. I had a notion that some of you didn't like my work, and this is a pretty convincing proof. I am very much obliged to you,' making a low bow.

'Dear, dear!' said the President [Sir Martin Archer Shee] to the head-carpenter, 'how came that picture amongst the outsiders? Bring it back; it must be admitted, of course.'

'No! it must not' said Constable; 'out it goes!' and in spite of apology and entreaty, out it went.

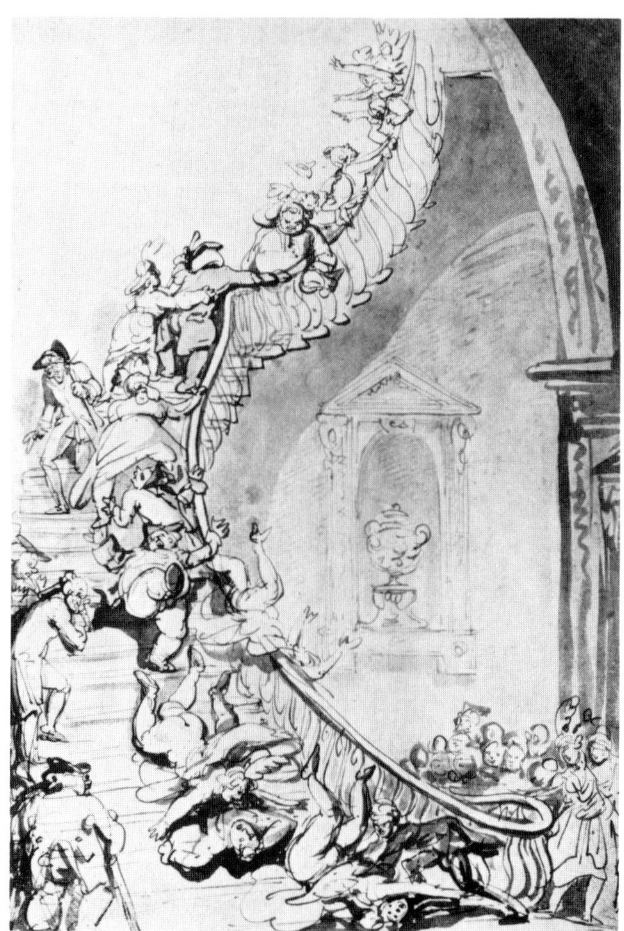

10
THOMAS ROWLANDSON
A Soirée at the Royal Academy (The Academy Stare-case), c. 1800
pen and ink, now destroyed

The pictures were hung in close proximity and made an astonishing, not to say confusing, display. The wall was divided by the *line,* a narrow wooden ledge about nine feet from the floor. Naturally, to be hung on or below the line at eye-level was of prime importance to the artists, for otherwise their works might not be noticed. Competition for this space was stiff and frequently led to fierce dispute: Gainsborough refused ever to show at the Academy again after 1784 when his portrait of *The Three Eldest Princesses* was hung above the line. Fearing that the poor light and distance would militate against public recognition of the subleties of handling and likeness in the work he withdrew it and all the others he had sent in that year. Similarly, in 1812 Turner threatened to withdraw his *Snow Storm: Hannibal and his Army Crossing the Alps* when it was hung above the line, for the picture's internal perspective would have been destroyed if it had been hung so high. Fortunately the work was re-hung. Joseph Wright of Derby had problems at the opposite end of the scale. He sent four pictures to the R.A. in 1784, but found that because they had been placed at the bottom of the wall they had been damaged by visitors' feet. The damage was doubtless compounded by the state of the floor which was covered by sawdust, kept down by daily watering. In the course of time a number of artists were to find themselves in conflict with the Academy over the hanging of their works, but artists are rarely satisfied and no system devised could be hoped to please everyone. Sometimes the 'skying' of pictures could even have benevolent side effects. In 1813, when Wilkie's *Blind Man's Buff* was 'picture of the year', the painter Thomas Stothard wrote to a friend:

> (it) has ever a crowd round it closely packed; and some of those in the rear, in vain struggling for a view, console themselves for the disappointment by looking upwards at my Shakespeare subject, by which means I get admirers, as one theatre is filled by the overflow of the other.

Close hanging of pictures could also lead to healthy rivalry. Turner, in particular, was very fond of heightening the effects of his paintings on Varnishing Days to show them to better advantage than their neighbours, though not always with successful results. George Jones recalled:

> *The View of Venice with Canaletti painting* [by Turner] hung ... next to a picture of mine which had a very blue sky. He [Turner] joked with me about it and threatened that if I did not alter it he would put it down by bright colour, which he was soon able to do by adding blue to his own ... and then went to work at some other picture. I enjoyed the joke and resolved to imitate it, and introduced a great deal more white into my sky, which made his look much

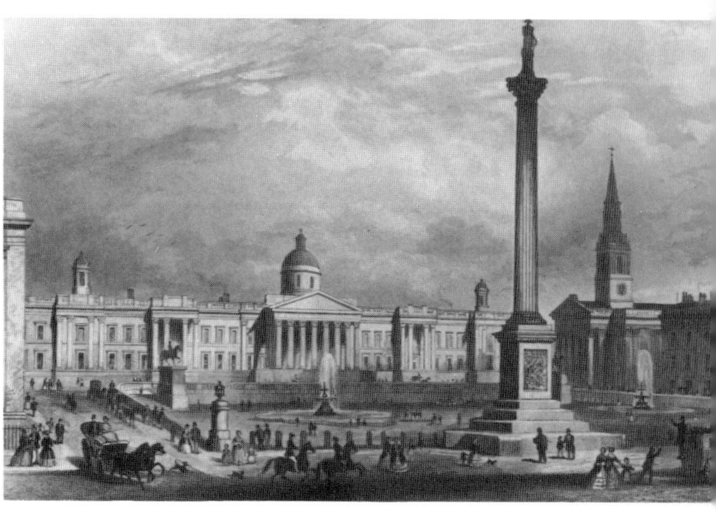

11
after THOMAS H. SHEPHERD
The National Gallery, London, 1850
The Royal Academy was housed in the right half of the building between 1837 and 1868.

> too blue. The ensuing day, he saw what I had done, laughed heartily, slapped my back and said I might enjoy the victory.

The Varnishing Days had been instituted in 1809 in order to prevent Members retouching works whenever they felt like it. Three (later five) days were allocated for this activity, immediately prior to the Private View. In the 1830s, Turner, who took particular advantage of them, often sent unfinished works which he would then complete within the period, to general amazement at his virtuosity. Although by the mid-century the usefulness of the five days given over to 'varnishing' was in doubt, they were retained in deference to Turner's artistic stature and they were only cut to two days after his death in 1851.

The Royal Academy continued to occupy the Fine Rooms in Somerset House until 1836, although over the years those premises became increasingly congested by the growing number of works being submitted for display. In addition, the government also required more space for offices on the site, and so in 1825 a Parliamentary committee was set up to investigate the problem. As the National Gallery (founded in 1824) also needed space, a decision was made in 1832 to house the two institutions

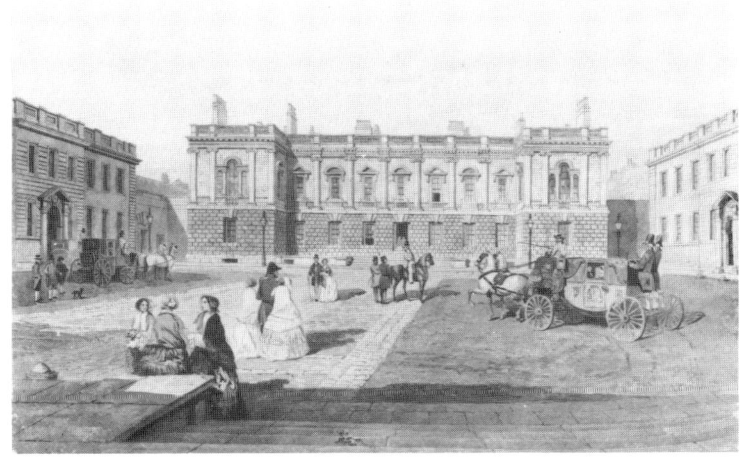

12
J.W.ARCHER
Old Burlington House; The Front, 1855
watercolour
British Museum, London

jointly on a site in Trafalgar Square (Ill. 11). William Wilkins designed the new building and in 1837 the Academy moved into five rooms in its eastern half. The new building immediately proved inadequate for its purpose. The rooms hardly matched those at Somerset House, and although they undoubtedly provided more space, it was still neccessary to exclude many works from the annual Exhibition. In 1850, steps were initiated to find other premises and eventually the decision was taken to convert a large mansion in Piccadilly (Ill. 12) into a permanent home for the Academy. Extensive alterations and additions were made and the first Exhibition was held at Burlington House in 1869.

Burlington House had originally been constructed in about 1664 for Richard Boyle, the 1st Earl of Burlington. The 3rd Earl came into possession of it in 1704, at the age of ten, and later, influenced by Palladian architecture, he had numerous alterations made by Colin Campbell, several of which are still apparent. The southern façade incorporates his changes, but the building was altered again around 1815 for Lord George Cavendish by Samuel Ware. It was bought by the Government in 1854 and leased to the Academy for 999 years at a peppercorn rent of £1 per year. Various conditions were attached to this generous arrangement. They included an obligation to retain the southern façade (though a third storey was added to match the height of a new courtyard) and the creation, by the Academy, of new exhibition galleries and schools to the north of the house on the site of the gardens. As a result,there are now seventeen main galleries, as well as two rows of studios which house the Schools. The colonnades in the original courtyard and the impressive gateway were demolished in 1867 during the rebuilding.

These premises were much more suitable for the by now greatly expanded annual Exhibition. Victorian prosperity and public interest in the arts were reflected in the number of works on show. In 1869 this consisted of some 1320 works chosen out of a submission of 4500 and there were 315,000 visitors. The greater space allowed for a less constricted hanging of pictures. By the 1880s attendance had increased to well over 400,000 visitors, an indication both of the growth of public interest in art and the greater part the Academy played in focussing that interest.

Old Master loan exhibitions were occasionally held in the winter months, but these were less well-attended than the summer exhibitions of contemporary art – an indication of how effectively in its first hundred years the Academy had altered taste since Hogarth's day. Gradually, the fashion for Old Masters, so lamented by Hogarth, had given way to a preference for works by living British artists. These artists expressed themselves in a number of traditions – history painting,portraiture, landscape, animal and genre painting – to which we must now turn our attention. Of course, to try to chart the whole history of British art as influenced by the Royal Academy is impossible in a short volume; the length and complexity of that history precludes such an attempt. But it is worthwhile to examine briefly the currents of thought and feeling that occupied many of the artists of the Royal Academy.

When the Royal Academy came into existence, it reflected a direct need in British society. Primarily, of course, it was created because a group of influential artists required a more prestigious and direct means of communication. The institution flourished immediately, however, because the Industrial Revolution was beginning to bring forth a new monied class for whom the acquisition of art was both a social obligation and a cultural necessity. The growth of leisure, education and literacy brought about by that revolution also led to a greater demand for art-education. The foundation of the Academy Schools contributed, in turn, to higher standards of artistic technique and so further increased the importance of the Academy's role in British cultural life. Fortuitously the French Revolution and the wars of 1793-1815 isolated Britain from Continental art soon after the Academy was founded, and this also called into being a greater demand for British art. The combination of these factors decisively stimulated the Royal Academy as the natural forcing-ground for a 'School of English Artists'.

By the time of its foundation the different categories of art that were to be explored in the Royal Academy over the following two centuries were already broadly determined. These categories were discussed by Sir Joshua Reynolds in his Discourses. Living in a culture that was supremely certain of its values, Reynolds had no hesitation in asserting a hierarchy in art, a classification of subjects graded according to purpose and inherent quality. Without doubt one such category reigned supreme over all others.

History Painting

When Sir Joshua delivered his Discourses during the early years of the Academy it was with the avowed intention of promoting a profoundly serious art. He required that an artist should

> instead of endeavouring to amuse mankind with the minute neatness of his imitations ... endeavour to improve them by the grandeur of his ideas; instead of seeking praise, by deceiving the superficial sense of the spectator, he must strive for fame by capturing the imagination.

For Reynolds this 'capturing' was to be achieved by the imparting of 'intellectual dignity' which would impress 'the appearance of philosophick wisdom or heroick virtue'; in short, the Great Style.

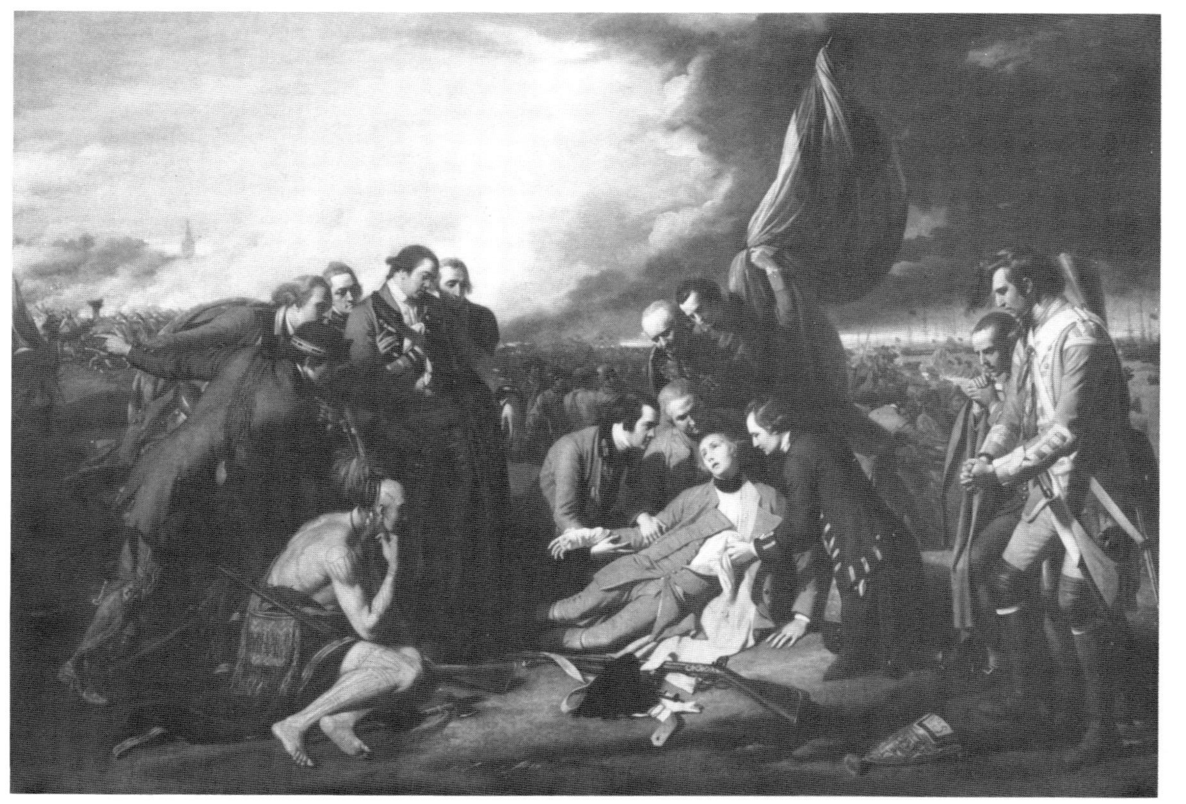

13
SIR BENJAMIN WEST, P.R.A.
The Death of Wolfe, R.A. 1771
oil on canvas, 151.1 × 213.3cm.(59½ × 84in.)
National Gallery of Canada, Ottawa
General James Wolfe was killed at the Battle of the Plains of Abraham, near Quebec, in which the British defeated

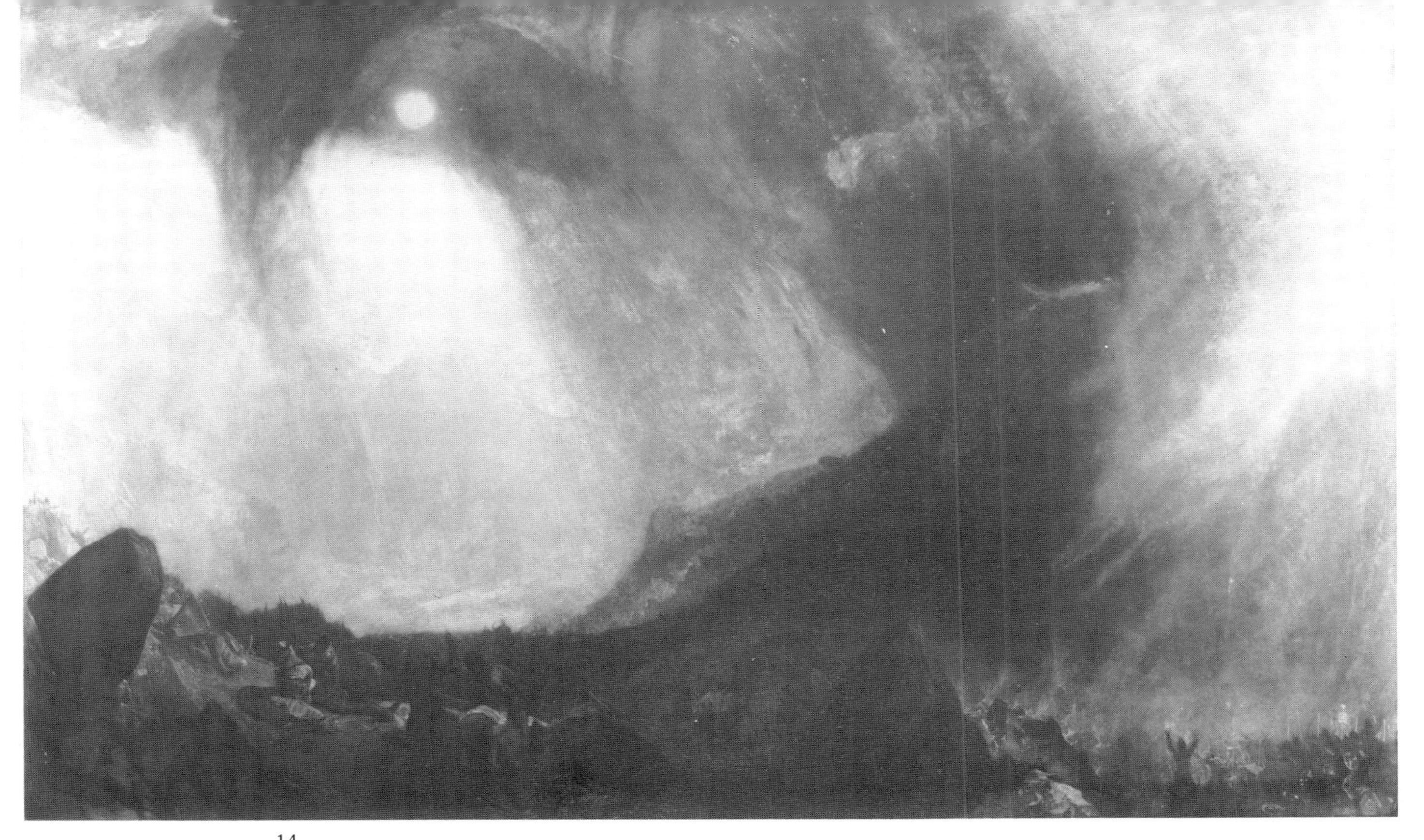

14
J.M.W. TURNER, R.A.
Snow Storm: Hannibal and his Army crossing the Alps,
R.A. 1812; oil on canvas, 146 X 237.5cm.(57½ X 93in.)
Tate Gallery, London

The natural vehicle for this attainment of dignity was 'history' painting, the representation of mythological, allegorical, religious, historical or literary subjects. Indeed, throughout the subsequent history of the Royal Academy it was pictures on precisely these themes that formed the artistic centre of gravity. For a great number of artists such as Reynolds, West, Barry, Copley, Rigaud, Hamilton, Wright of Derby, Danby, De Loutherbourg, Turner, Haydon, Maclise, Egg, Frith, the Pre-Raphaelites, Poynter and Alma-Tadema (and even in our own day Spencer) history subjects were the vehicles for the most serious and elevated efforts.

Paintings of themes derived from classical mythology were much to the taste of the eighteenth-century aristocracy, who were later aped in this by the industrial middle-class. It was a predilection produced by an educational system based largely upon the Classics, and it fitted in with the greater cosmos that the aristocracy wished to create. In private city squares or country houses and parks, they wished to see a reconstruction of the classical past. They felt that Britain, or at least their Britain, was the heir to that past. From the Greek or Roman scenes on their walls they could look through neo-classical windows on to a landscape that was organised to make those dream-worlds a reality. Allegory was a natural offshoot of this awareness, for it allowed comment upon the present through the guise of classicism. Increasingly, religious art was to meet the needs of a fervour stoked by the physical, spiritual and psychological dislocations of the Industrial Revolution. Literary painting offered a natural choice of subject-matter to literate painters who were also highly aware of the growing literacy of their public. Fuseli commented wryly:

> The Englishman eats roast beef and plum pudding, drinks port or claret; therefore, if you will be read by him, you must open the portals of Hell with the hand of Milton, convulse his ear or his sides with Shakespeare's buskin or sock, raise him above the stars with Dryden's Cecilia or sink him to the grave with the melancholy of Gray.

Patriotism, self-esteem, moral and spiritual certainty, all of these could be essayed through *Istoria*. Today, of course, this type of art is generally despised (and much of it rightly so), for it seldom transcends the limitations of its content to achieve a universal human statement; most often it merely 'illustrates' its subject. But in the finest examples of the tradition, paintings such as Benjamin West's *The Death of Wolfe* (R.A.1771,Ill.13), Turner's *Snow Storm: Hannibal and his Army crossing the Alps* (R.A. 1812, Ill. 14) and *Dido building Carthage; or the Rise of the Carthaginian Empire* (R.A. 1815, Plate III) or Fuseli's *Lady Macbeth seizing the daggers* (R.A. 1812, Ill. 15) history painting imparted very profound values indeed.

West's *The Death of Wolfe* marked a high point in the tradition. It is probably the most famous of all British eighteenth-century history paintings and the fact that it is a completely inaccurate depiction of events is entirely beside the point. In reality there were probably only four or five people present when Wolfe died – and only one of those characters is represented by West. This does not detract from his achievement. The painting was an archetypal image for its age, a picture that touched a deep chord in the popular consciousness. West based the composition upon the traditional schema for the deposition of Christ and this device invests the picture, by association, with a dignity and symbolism that greatly contributed to its widespread appeal. West went on to paint three further versions of it and the picture very probably clarified Reynolds' ideas on contemporary history painting.

Naturally, subjects like the death of Wolfe greatly appealed to patriotic sentiment, and in a period of frequent wars and revolutions, such themes often appeared at the Academy. Some were miserable failures: West's *Queen Elizabeth going in procession to St. Paul's Cathedral after the Destruction of the Spanish Armada* (R.A. 1794, Ill. 16) is an unhappy hotchpotch of regurgitated Elizabethan research that was clearly exhibited to bolster the spirits of an England at war with France.

Turner's *Hannibal* (Ill. 14), however, projects a statement about the fate of nations on a much more significant level. One of Turner's great achievements, of course, was to 'raise' landscape painting to the status of history painting, and here the historical subject is combined with a penetrating observation of natural phenomena. The result transforms the use of history as a means of commenting upon contemporary events. By its timing and subject, Turner equates Hannibal and Napoleon. A similar depth of meaning is contained in *Dido building Carthage* (Plate III), in which a sunrise may allude to the arrival of peace after the

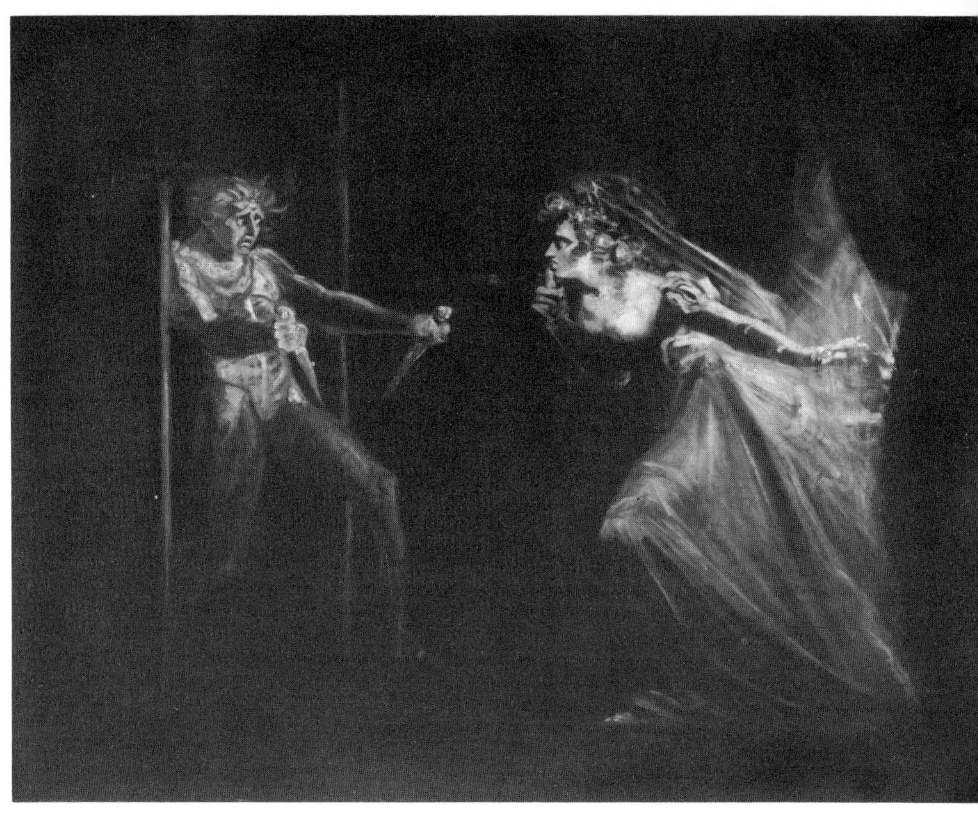

15
HENRI FUSELI, R.A.
Lady Macbeth seizing the daggers, R.A. 1812
oil on canvas, 101 × 127cm.(39¾ × 50in.)
Tate Gallery, London

long Napoleonic wars and the buildings under construction herald the dawn of a new age of peace and prosperity.

Fuseli's *Lady Macbeth seizing the daggers* (Ill. 15) is a good example of how successful history painting could be when it subordinated its subject to the demands of pictorial imagination. By using the innate expressiveness of paint to heighten the dramatic effect the picture becomes an equivalent to the text and not merely its illustration.

A branch of history painting that was particularly popular in the Academy was one that treated of religious themes and the coming of the Millenium. To the industrial poor in the early nineteenth century the advent of the Industrial Revolution had

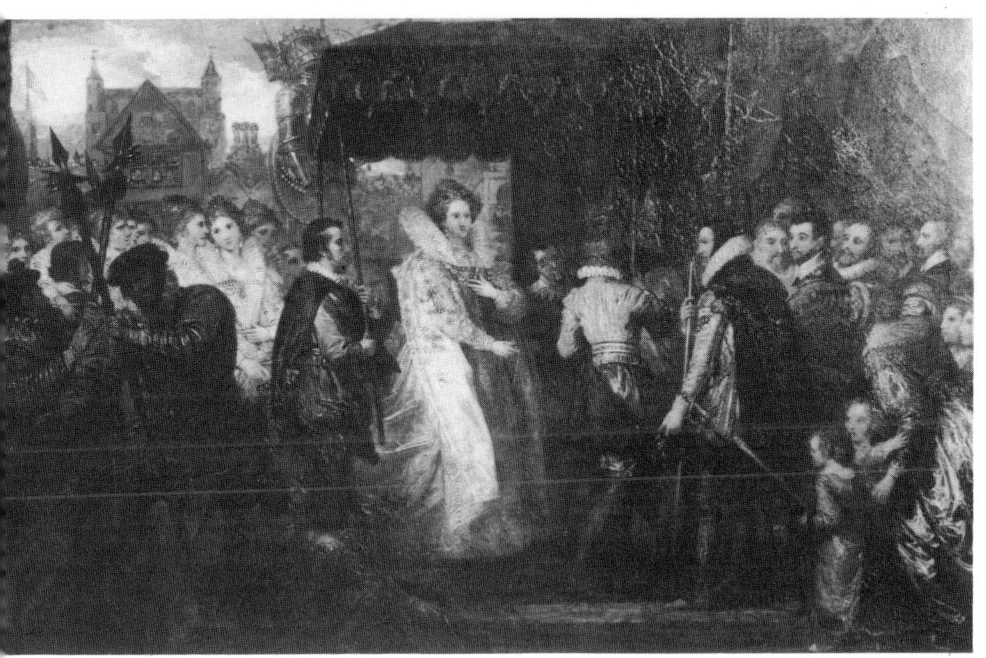

16
SIR BENJAMIN WEST, P.R.A.
Queen Elizabeth going in procession to St Paul's Cathedral after the Destruction of the Spanish Armada, 1792, R.A. 1794
oil on canvas, 43.1 × 66cm.(17 × 26in.)
Present whereabouts unknown
·st based the portrait of Elizabeth I on an engraving
·r Nicholas Hilliard.

meant dispossession from an agrarian stability that had lasted for centuries. Those vast and ever-growing tumours of the age, the industrial cities, seemed to portend the end of the world. Fundamental Christianity has always flourished among the oppressed and this was no less true in 'Satanic' England than in ancient Rome. Artists responded to this tension. Francis Danby's *The Delivery of Israel out of Egypt* (R.A. 1825, Ill. 17) is a scene of judgement, depicting the forces of good and evil in a way that captured some measure of the gloom of the new age. Equally apposite to their time were the enormous and terrifying sermons of John Martin. The first work Martin exhibited at the Academy, *Sadak in search of the waters of Oblivion* (R.A. 1812, Ill. 18), seems an archetypal Romantic image, a titanic landscape that dwarfs its solitary figure. Martin's later pictures were frequently exhibited outside the Academy and their images of Divine intervention

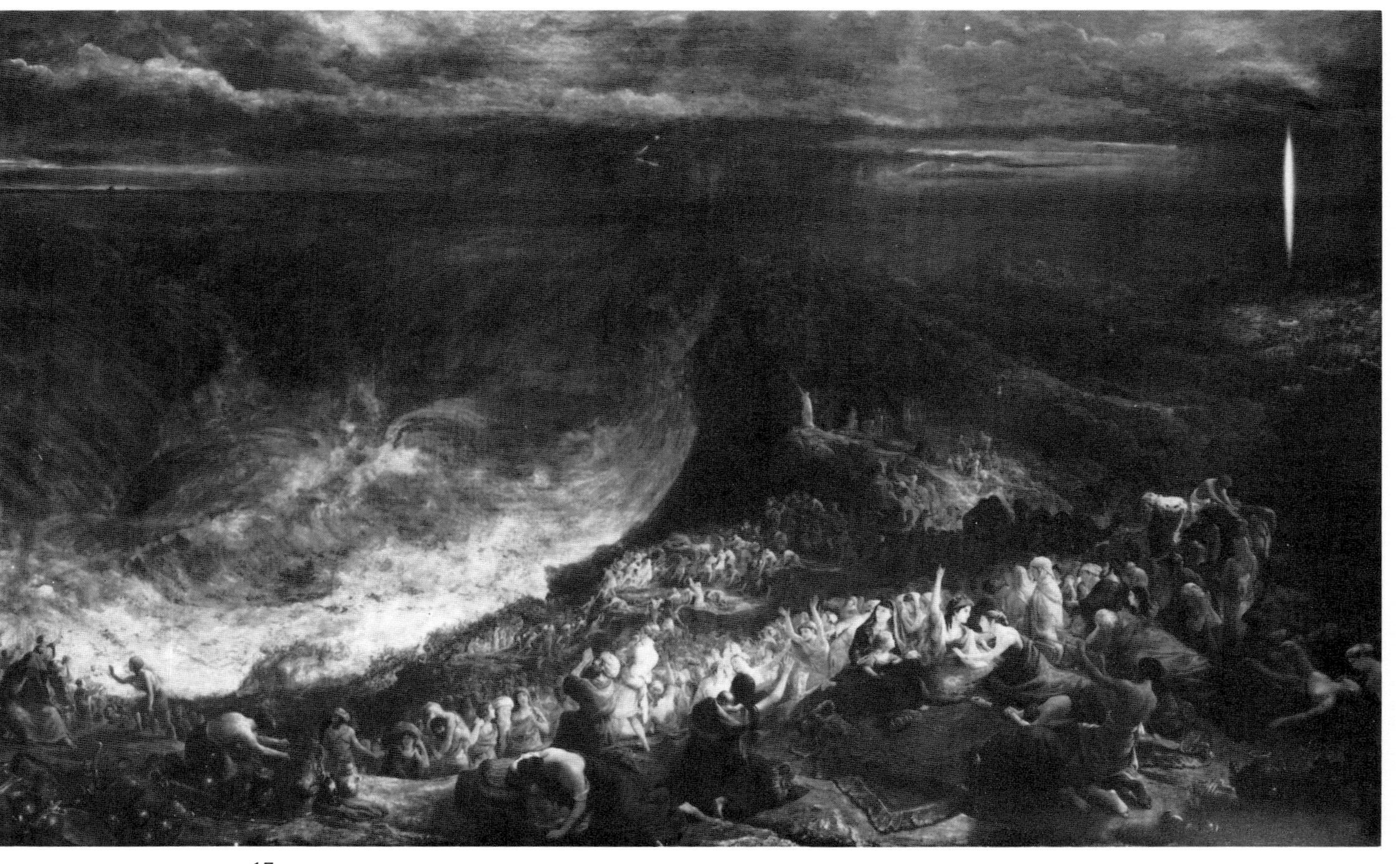

17
FRANCIS DANBY, A.R.A.
The Delivery of Israel out of Egypt, R.A. 1825
oil on canvas, 149.2 × 239.3cm.(58¾ × 94½in.)

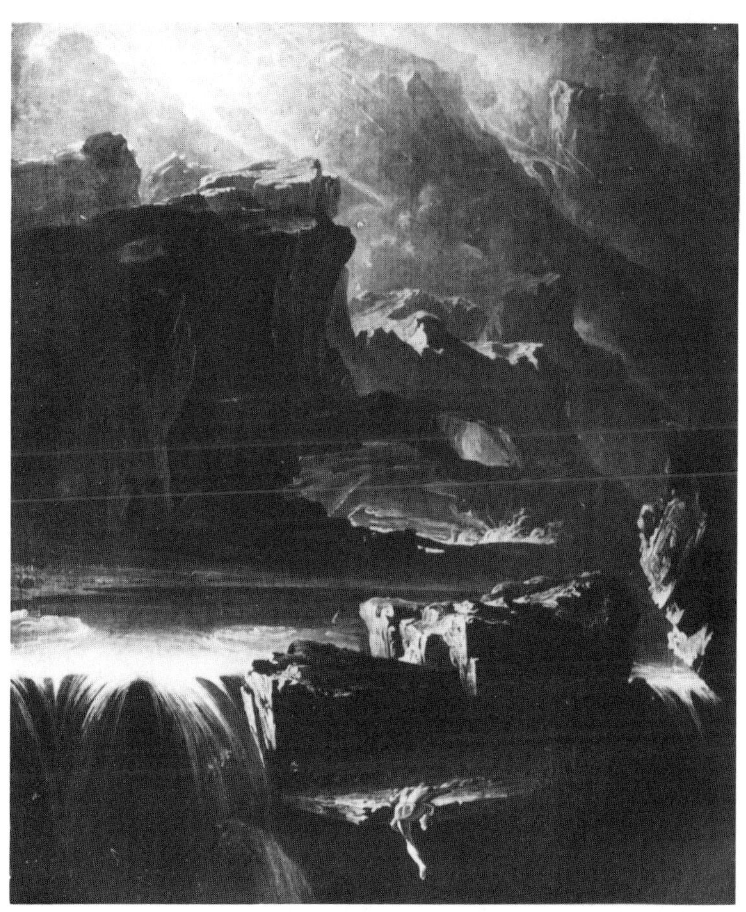

18
JOHN MARTIN
Sadak in search of the Waters of Oblivion
oil on canvas, 76.2 × 63.5cm.(30 × 25in.)
Southampton Art Gallery
s is a smaller version of the first painting exhibited by rtin at the Royal Academy in 1812, the whereabouts of ch are now unknown. The subject is taken from *Tales of Genii,* translated by James Ridley.

seem increasingly disturbing today, redolent as they are of the same kind of morbid neurosis that is typified in Wesley's hymn:

> Ah, lovely Appearance of Death
> No sight upon Earth is so fair!
> Not all the gay Pageants that *breathe*
> Can with a dead Body compare.

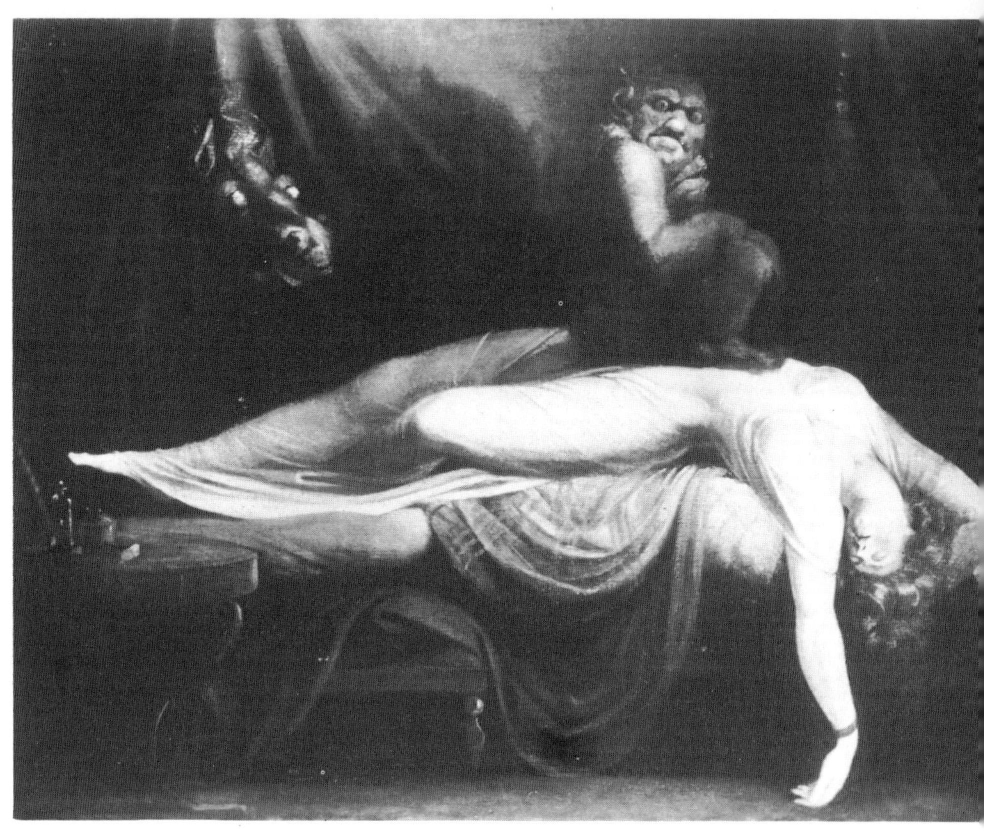

19
HENRY FUSELI, R.A.
The Nightmare, 1781, R.A. 1782
oil on canvas, 101 × 124.5cm.(39¾ × 49in.)
Detroit Institute of Arts, Detroit, U.S.A.

Seen in this light Fuseli's pictures present us with a far more healthy form of psychological disturbance. Swiss-born (his real name was Johann Heinrich Füssli), Henry Fuseli was ordained as a Zwinglian Minister but soon abandoned the Church for painting. After travelling around Europe he settled in London in 1779. He became an Academician in 1790, the Professor of painting in 1799 and Keeper in 1804. He retained the latter post until his death in 1825. Fuseli created a sensation at the Academy in 1782 with his painting *The Nightmare* (Ill. 19). This picture (a print of which is reputed to have hung in Freud's waiting-room) is an archetypal sexual image, the woman stretched out in the most langorous position possible, the incubus (or nightmare)

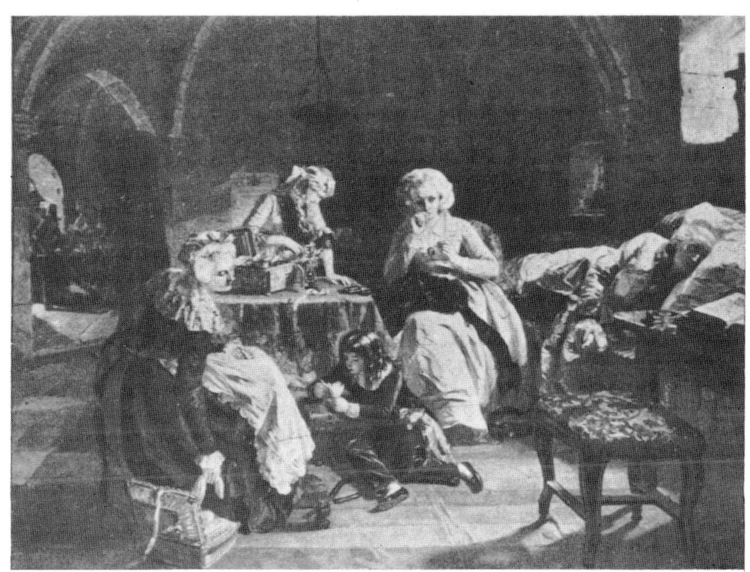

20
EDWARD MATTHEW WARD, R.A.
The Royal Family of France in the Prison of the Temple, R.A. 1851
oil on canvas, 101 × 127cm.(40 × 50in.)
Harris Art Gallery, Preston, Lancs. U.K.

squatting over her womb and a wildly-staring horse perhaps acting as a symbol of sexual drive.

Fuseli was a highly original artist whose work displays obvious affinities with Blake. Instead of Blake's intense religiosity, however, Fuseli created a much more phantasmagoric and secular universe, one that points the way toward twentieth century surrealism with its similar emphasis upon subconscious imagery.

Yet with time, and the growth of Victorian materialism, history painting was diluted. It became historicism, a very different artistic preoccupation altogether. History painting as envisaged by Reynolds embodied a high aesthetic and moral purpose; historicism came to signify copious research, shallow moralism and complete escapism. Indeed, the nineteenth century saw Reynolds' lofty aspirations for history painting gradually submerge into a sea of bathos. This growth of superficial feeling is easily seen in pictures such as E.M.Ward's *The Royal Family of France in the Prison of the Temple* (R.A. 1851, Ill. 20) or Edward Poynter's *Israel in Egypt* (R.A.1867, Ill.21). Both were 'pictures of the year' when they were exhibited, as *The Death of*

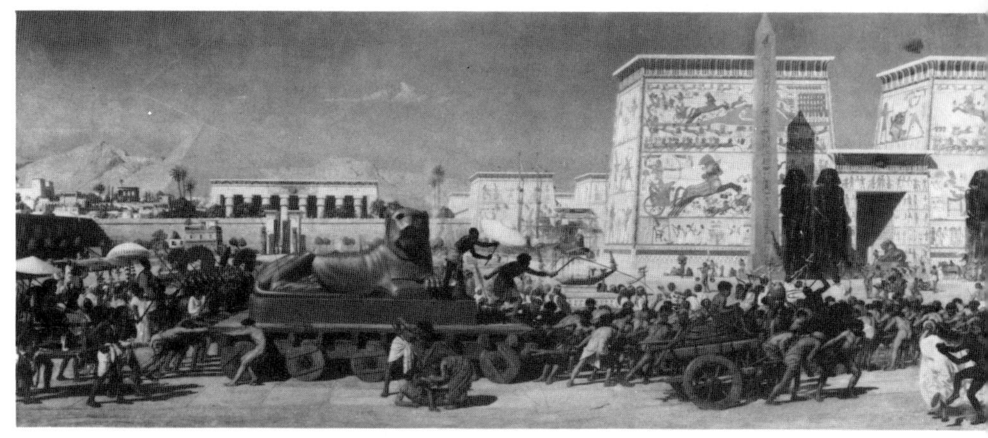

21
SIR EDWARD POYNTER, P.R.A.
Israel in Egypt, R.A. 1867
oil on canvas, 137.1 × 317.5cm(54 × 125in.)
Guildhall Art Gallery, London

Wolfe had been, but Ward's painting relies entirely upon historic verisimilitude and cheap sentiment for its effect. The Poynter is little better, although it displays a convincing evocation of Eastern light and colour. What is missing from both works, and they are masterpieces compared with some 'pictures of the year', is any degree of authentic human experience or formal invention that would give them some permanent significance. Such criticisms can also be levelled at the works of the Pre-Raphaelites, many of which were exhibited at the Royal Academy (Ill. 22). Despite an innovatory use of colour, meticulous craftsmanship and endless 'truthfulness' of appearance, they share the same limitations. The subjects dictated that lived experience should be sacrificed on the altar of pictorial rhetoric. The Pre-Raphaelites painted fine landscape studies but filled them with sentimental platitudes. The absence of the desire to fuse emotional and formal elements was to prove a fatal omission; it was compounded by the substitution of the studio for reality, of conceptual ideas for perceptual experience.

Ultimately, of course, Pre-Raphaelitism (which in any case was a movement born in almost total ignorance of Italian painting before Raphael) was swallowed up in the tide of Victorian historical painting and often came to embody its worst features. Only in recent times has history painting been convincingly resurrected in the works of Stanley Spencer and this because the

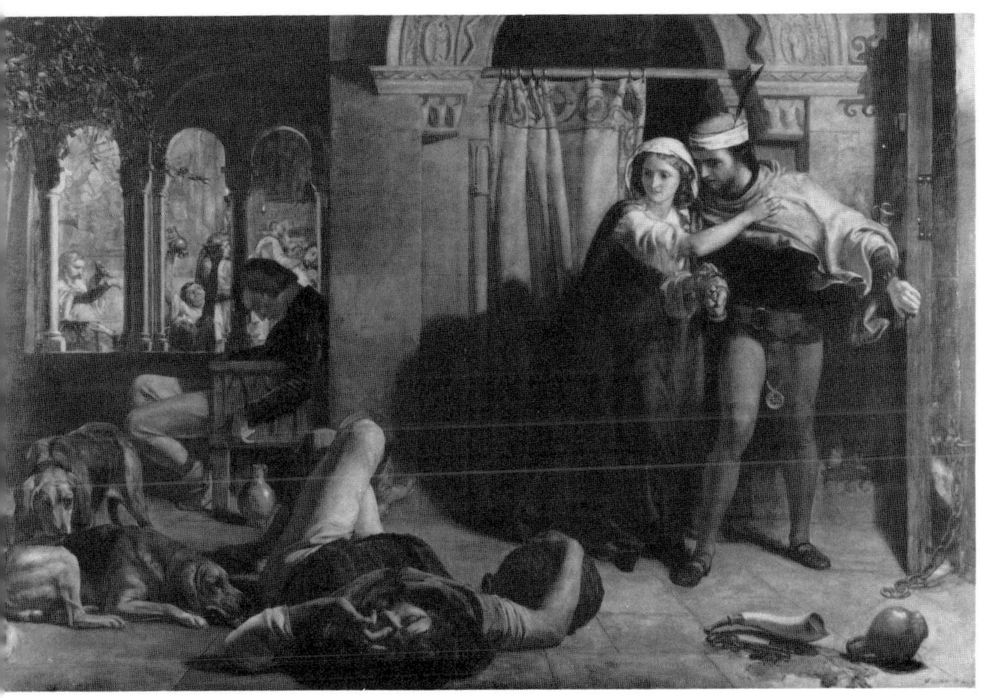

22
WILLIAM HOLMAN HUNT
The Flight of Madeline and Porphyro during the drunkeness attending the revelry, R.A.1848
oil on canvas, 77.4 × 113cm.(30½ × 44½in.)
Guildhall Art Gallery, London
‹e subject is taken from *The Eve of St. Agnes* by Keats.

roots of his art lay in genuine human, spiritual and above all *pictorial* values. For the rest, the tradition of British history painting has been a rather empty one, with artists drawing upon enormous energies and resources to bring forth vacuous works that are impressive only for their technical accomplishment.

Portraiture

Reynolds' own attempts at history painting were among his least successful efforts. Yet when he combined his aspirations in this sphere with his more usual vehicle, portraiture, the results could be dazzling. His portrayal of the three daughters of Sir William Montgomery as *Three Ladies adorning a Term of Hymen* (R.A. 1774, Ill. 23) was regarded by the artist as 'the best picture I ever painted.' Here Reynolds brought together portraiture and allegory, for the work not only celebrates female beauty but also the institution of marriage. One of the sisters was newly wed at the time, the second on the verge of marriage and the third extremely eligible. The married sister has 'passed' the God of Wedlock and is encircled by a wreath of flowers; another approaches the God while the third still picks the flowers. By this means a study of three women is directed towards greater 'philosophick' ends.

This masterpiece represents the grandiose, classicizing end of Reynolds' scale. He could also create 'fancy' pictures where he relaxed his lofty sense of purpose. *The Strawberry Girl* (R.A. 1773, Ill. 24) shows the other side of his personality, one that was easy-going, playful and capable of great affection. The picture is undeniably sentimental, but it lacks the cloying qualities of similar pictures of children by later artists (such as Millais' *Bubbles*).

Such charming works are mere chippings from the painter who may be considered the supreme aesthetic arbiter of his age in Britain. Reynolds possessed enviable intellectual powers and they were sharpened by contact with some of the greatest minds of the day. He numbered among his close friends men such as Johnson and Burke, Sheridan and Goldsmith. Reynolds was conscious of his artistic authority and he clearly represents this in his *Self Portrait as D.C.L.* (Frontispiece). He received his Honorary Doctorate of Civil Law from Oxford University in 1773 and the portrait directly refers to Rembrandt's *Aristotle contemplating a bust of*

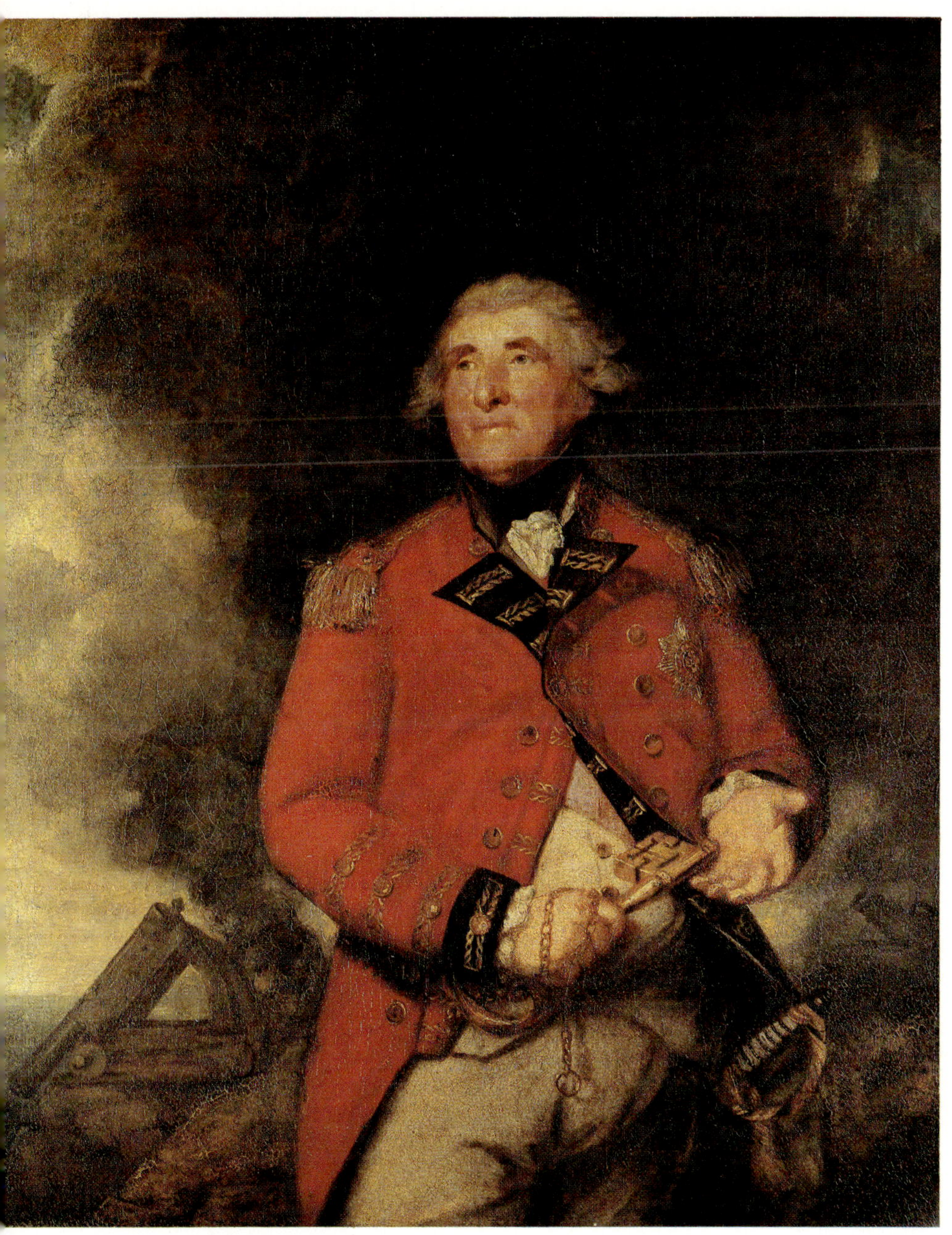

Plate I
SIR JOSHUA REYNOLDS P.R.A.
George Augustus Elliot, Lord Heathfield
R.A. 1788
oil on canvas, 142 × 114cm.(56 × 44¾in.)
National Gallery, London

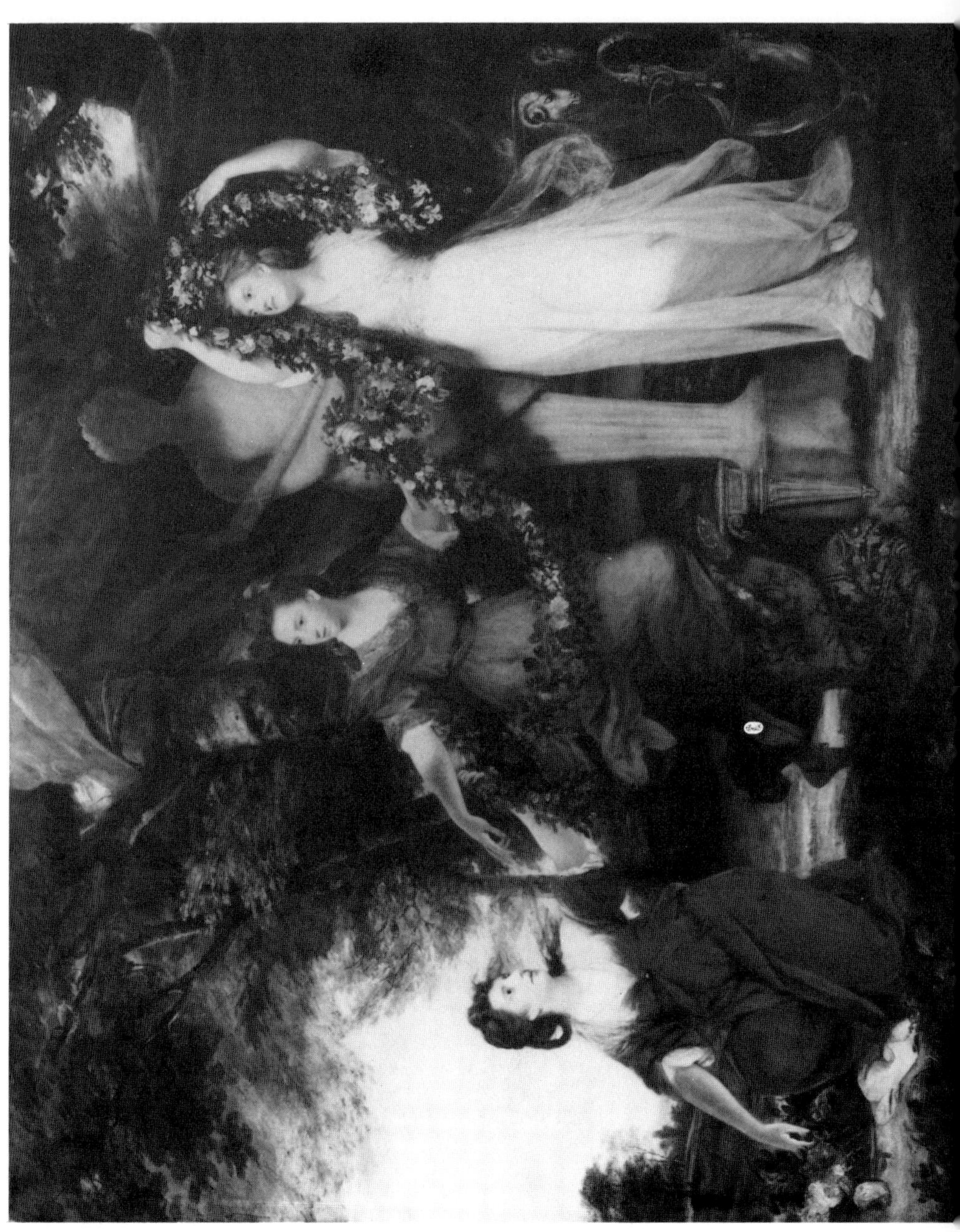

Three Ladies adorning a Term of Hymen, R.A. 1774
oil on canvas, 234 × 295cm.(92 × 116⅛in.)
Tate Gallery, London

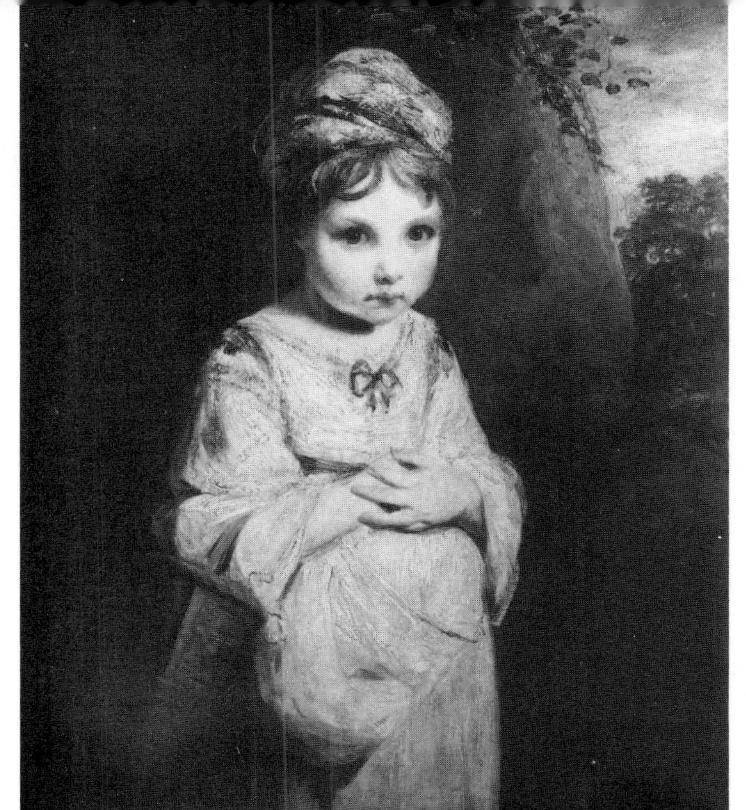

24
SIR JOSHUA REYNOLDS, P.R.A.
The Strawberry Girl, R.A. 1773
oil on canvas, 74 × 63cm.(30 × 25in.)
Wallace Collection, London
The model was probably the painter's niece, Offy Palmer.

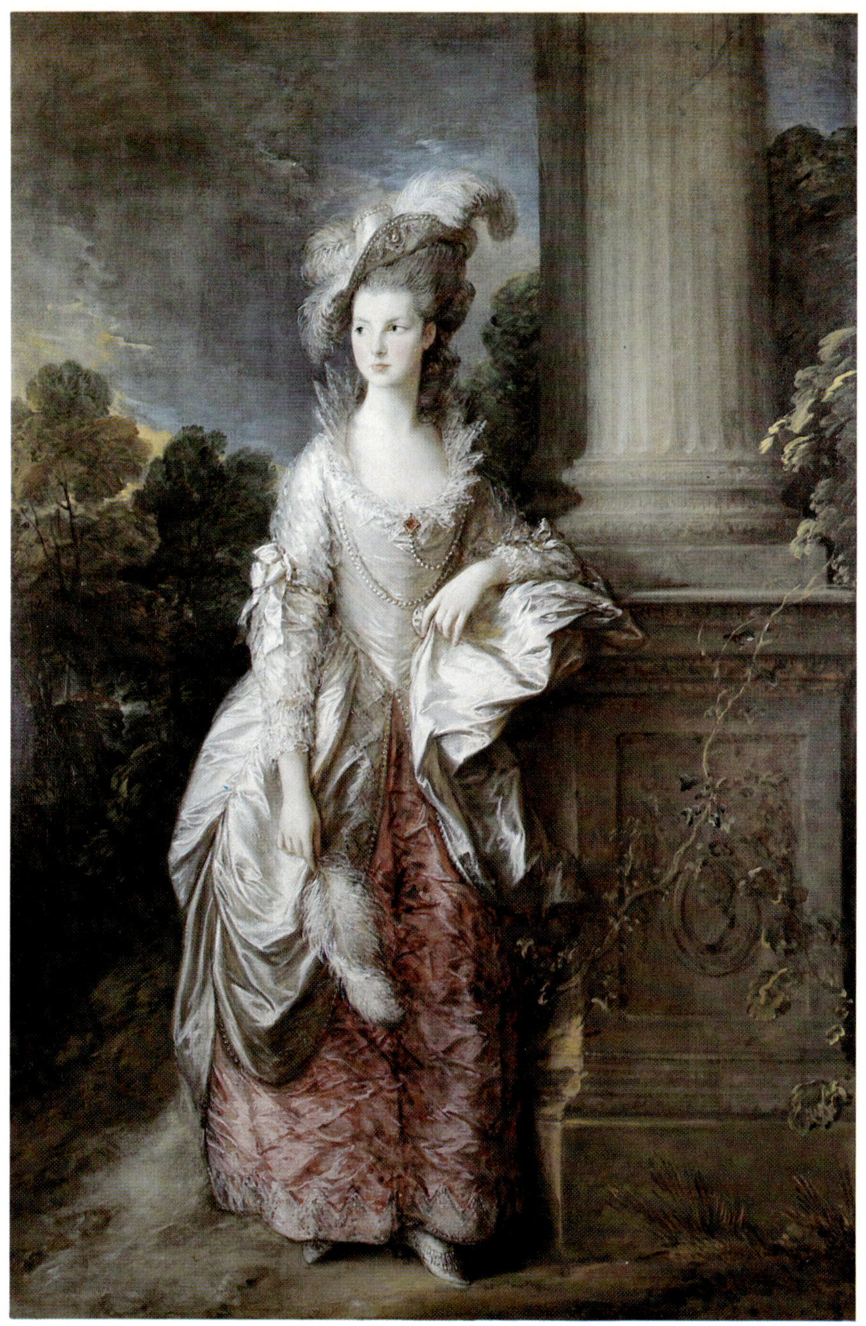

Plate II
THOMAS GAINSBOROUGH, R.A.
The Hon. Mrs. Thomas Graham
R.A. 1777
oil on canvas, 236.2 × 154.3cm.(93½ × 60¾in.)
National Gallery of Scotland, Edinburgh

Homer, for Reynolds places a bust of his great exemplar, Michelangelo, in the picture. The reference to Rembrandt is typical of Reynolds for whom painting was an activity that constantly renewed and enriched itself through contact with the greatest art of the past. By such means as quotation or by the use of formal devices used by previous masters, Reynolds profoundly enhanced his powers of pictorial invention. In his greatest works he also achieves a complete fusion of form and content, always taking pains to impart a sense of social and psychological status to his sitters. Thus the masterful portrait of *George Augustus Elliot, Lord Heathfield* (R.A. 1788, Plate I) is entirely dedicated to expressing nobility of character. General Elliot had been the defender of Gibraltar against the Spanish between 1779 and1782. Reynolds depicts him holding the keys to the Rock and quite naturally surrounds him with 'the clouds of war'. On either side are guns that buttress the composition. By the adoption of a low viewpoint and the use of a triangular composition to provide unity, the portrait suggests the General's dignity and resolution in adversity.

Throughout Reynolds' *oeuvre* such a monumentality of scale is frequently in evidence and it undoubtedly reflects the aggrandizing tendency of history painting. However, Reynolds' great rival as a portraitist, Thomas Gainsborough, did not share the President's attitude towards *Istoria.* He commented upon the Fourth Discourse that

> Sir Joshua either forgets, or does not chuse to see that his instruction is all adapted to form the History-Painter, which he must know there is no call for in this country

Gainsborough was wrong, for there was a great and growing demand for such work. Nonetheless, the comment indicates his own lack of interest in those productions. He preferred to concentrate his efforts upon what came naturally to him. Gainsborough was a founder-Member of the Academy and although his relations with the institution were stormy, some of his finest pictures were exhibited there before 1784. The portrait of *The Hon. Mrs Thomas Graham* (R.A. 1777, Plate II) is an example which embodies all the greatest qualities of Gainsborough's genius – his psychological insight, painterly virtuosity and sensitive feeling for form and colour. The shining satins and silks,

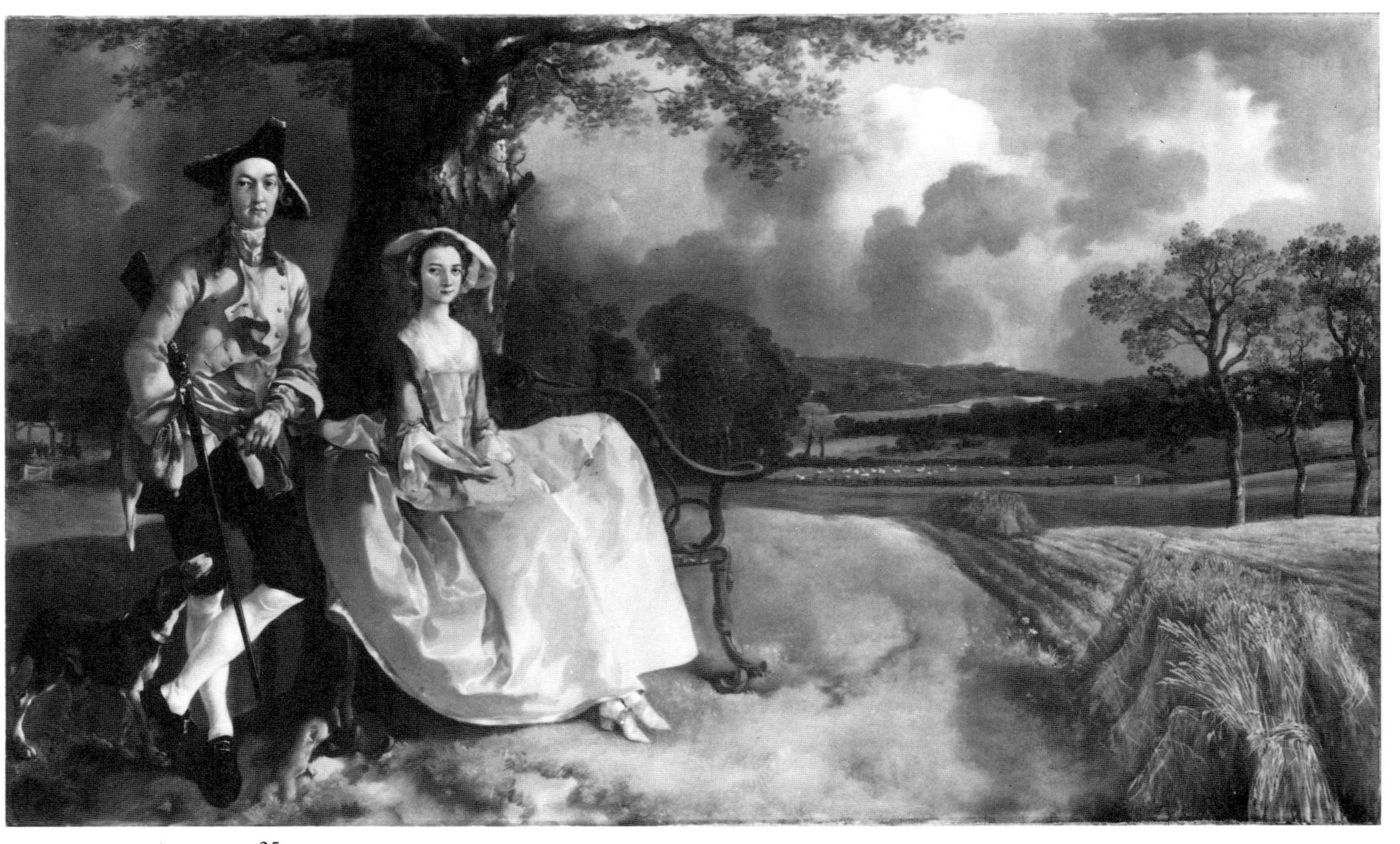

25
THOMAS GAINSBOROUGH, R.A.
Mr. and Mrs. Robert Andrews, 1749
oil on canvas, 69.8 × 119.3cm($27\frac{1}{2}$ × 47in.)
National Gallery, London

the contrast between such rich materials and flesh, stone, foliage and evanescent light, the stately, even imperious stance and glance, and the dashing reiteration of zigzag forms all combine to create a painting of breathtaking vivacity and power.

In Gainsborough's portraits we see the eighteenth century aristocracy as it wished to see itself - infinitely graceful and refined, cultured and immutably fixed in social status. Yet Gainsborough had an ambivalent attitude towards portraiture, occasionally damning his sitters and longing to devote himself to landscape, a genre for which there was little demand at the time. He felt that landscape was his true *metier,* and if his aspirations towards this branch of art remained largely unfulfilled, at least his appreciation of nature was occasionally incorporated into his portraits. The early *Mr and Mrs Robert Andrews of* 1749 (Ill. 25) is perhaps the finest open-air portrait painted in England. It observes a precise and happy balance between mankind and nature, establishing not only the social standing of the sitters but also their relationship to the rural world in which they lived. This natural emphasis was later to be pushed into the background of the portraits, but Gainsborough always achieved an exact equilibrium between man and the world, between subject and context.

His portraits also incorporate another major influence, namely music. Gainsborough was an enthusiastic musician and he was friendly with some of the finest composers and performers of the day, notably the youngest son of Johann Sebastian Bach, Johann Christian, the 'London' Bach. The influence of music can be easily discerned in the structure of the portrait of *Johann Christian Fischer* (R.A. 1780, Ill. 26). Fischer was a composer, the leading oboeist of his day and Gainsborough's son-in-law. The arabesque running up through the figure and along the edge of the curtain establishes a central rhythmic line which is counterpointed elsewhere. Apparent too is Gainsborough's response to character, the facial expression embodying the musician's spiritual elevation.

An even more daring fusion of portraiture, landscape and music is effected in *Giovanna Baccelli* (R.A. 1782, Ill. 27). Here the great ballet dancer's character is described with wit and verve. In addition to the charming expressiveness of the features, Gainsborough creates a unifying line along the raised hem of her decorative apron. This line is repeated by the edges of the cloud and given an added sense of roundness by the tambourine in the

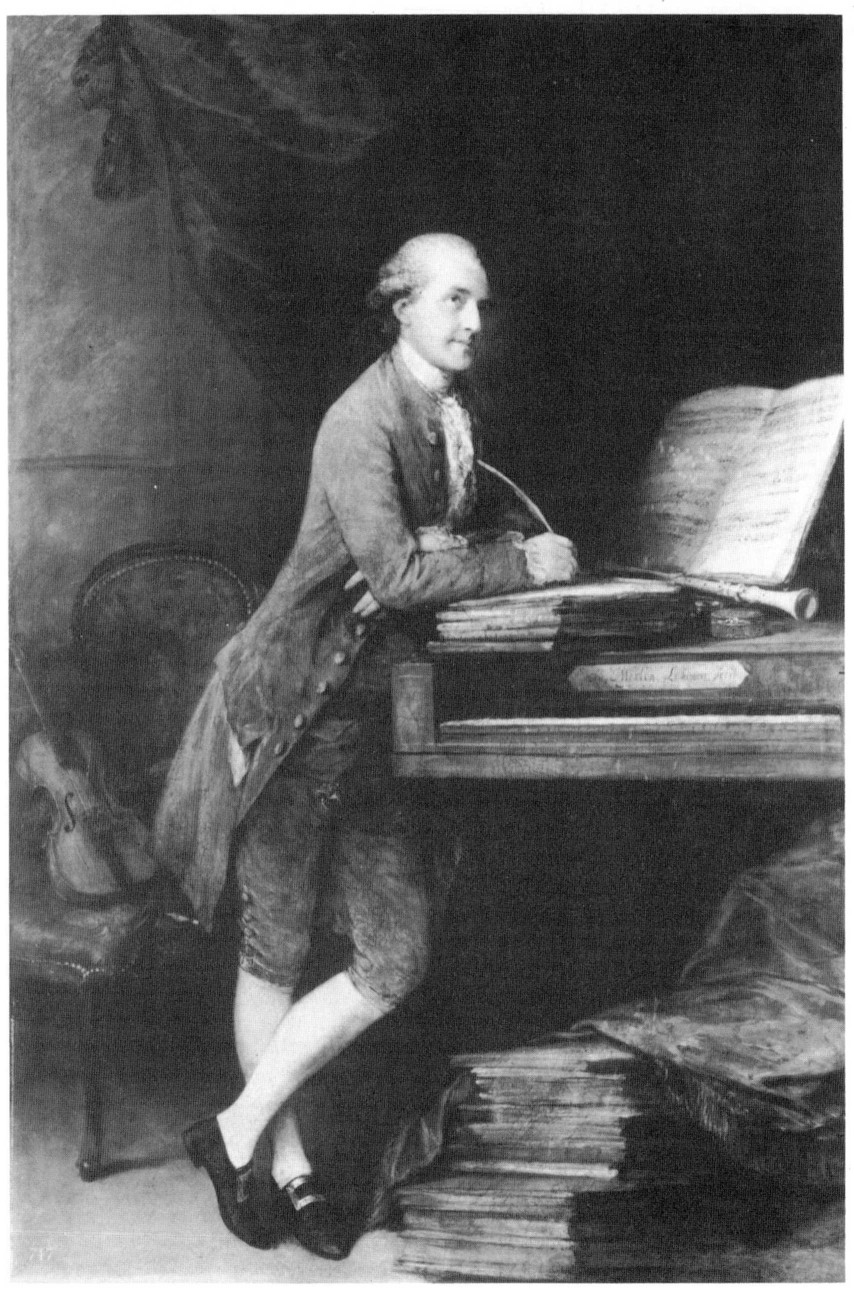

26
THOMAS GAINSBOROUGH, R.A.
Johann Christian Fischer, R.A. 1780
oil on canvas, 228.6 × 150.4cm.(90 × 59¼in.)
Buckingham Palace, London
(reproduced by gracious permission of Her Majesty the Queen)

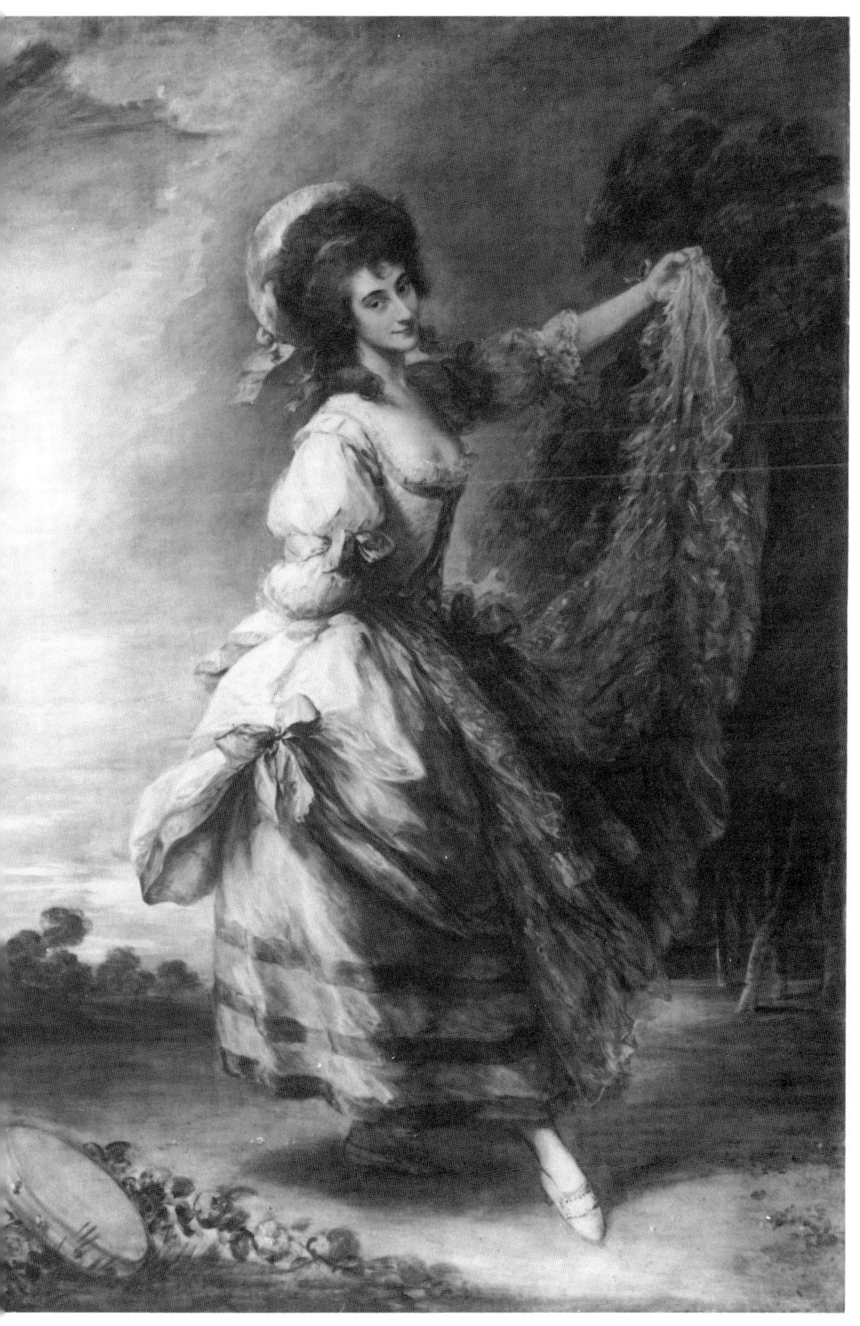

27
THOMAS GAINSBOROUGH, R.A.
Giovanna Bacelli, R.A. 1782
oil on canvas, 224.7 × 144.7cm.(88½ × 57in.)
Tate Gallery, London

bottom left-hand corner. The colours also produce a harmony analogous to music and, throughout, the vitality of Gainsborough's brush-work allows the whole picture to dance.

Gainsborough's landscapes are discussed below, but one other side of his character must be considered here. For Gainsborough nature was not passive. It was certainly an environment for peaceful human relationships but it also observed certain vital laws of its own. A painting exhibited at the Royal Academy in 1783 (Ill. 28) forcefully demonstrates this awareness. *The two shepherd boys with dogs fighting* reveals a vein of savagery in Gainsborough that seems all the more affecting because it comes from such a usually placid temperament. Gainsborough's comments to Sir William Chambers that 'I believe next exhibition I shall make the Boys fighting and the Dogs looking on – you know my cunning way of avoiding great subjects in Painting...' can be taken with a pinch of salt. Gainsborough here reveals the underlying cruelty of nature and in this respect directly anticipates the Romantic approach to the world. To earlier generations of artists, nature had appeared as essentially benevolent. For later Romantic artists such as Turner, Nature was fundamentally hostile, and that hostility was often the sole subject of their work. In this extraordinary painting Gainsborough directly anticipates that reaction. His understanding of mankind's related capacity for both pain and pleasure is indicated by the responses of the boys, one compassionate, the other enjoying the savage spectacle. They act as an inevitable reminder of Horace Walpole's dictum, formulated in 1769, that 'the world is a comedy to those that think, a tragedy to those that feel.'

The foundation of the Academy occurred near the end of Gainsborough's life, and his attitude towards the institution meant that he received little benefit from it. This cannot be said of the portraitist who might be regarded as his natural successor, Thomas Lawrence. Born to the manner of a Society portraitist, Lawrence was self-assured, polished, charming and hugely talented. He rose rapidly to fame: while Reynolds was still alive he was called 'the Sir Joshua of Futurity', and following Reynolds' death he became the Painter in Ordinary to the King. By the age of twenty-five he was an Academician and he later succeeded West as President. His portrait of *Queen Charlotte* (R.A. 1790, Ill. 29) immediately established his reputation and it is not

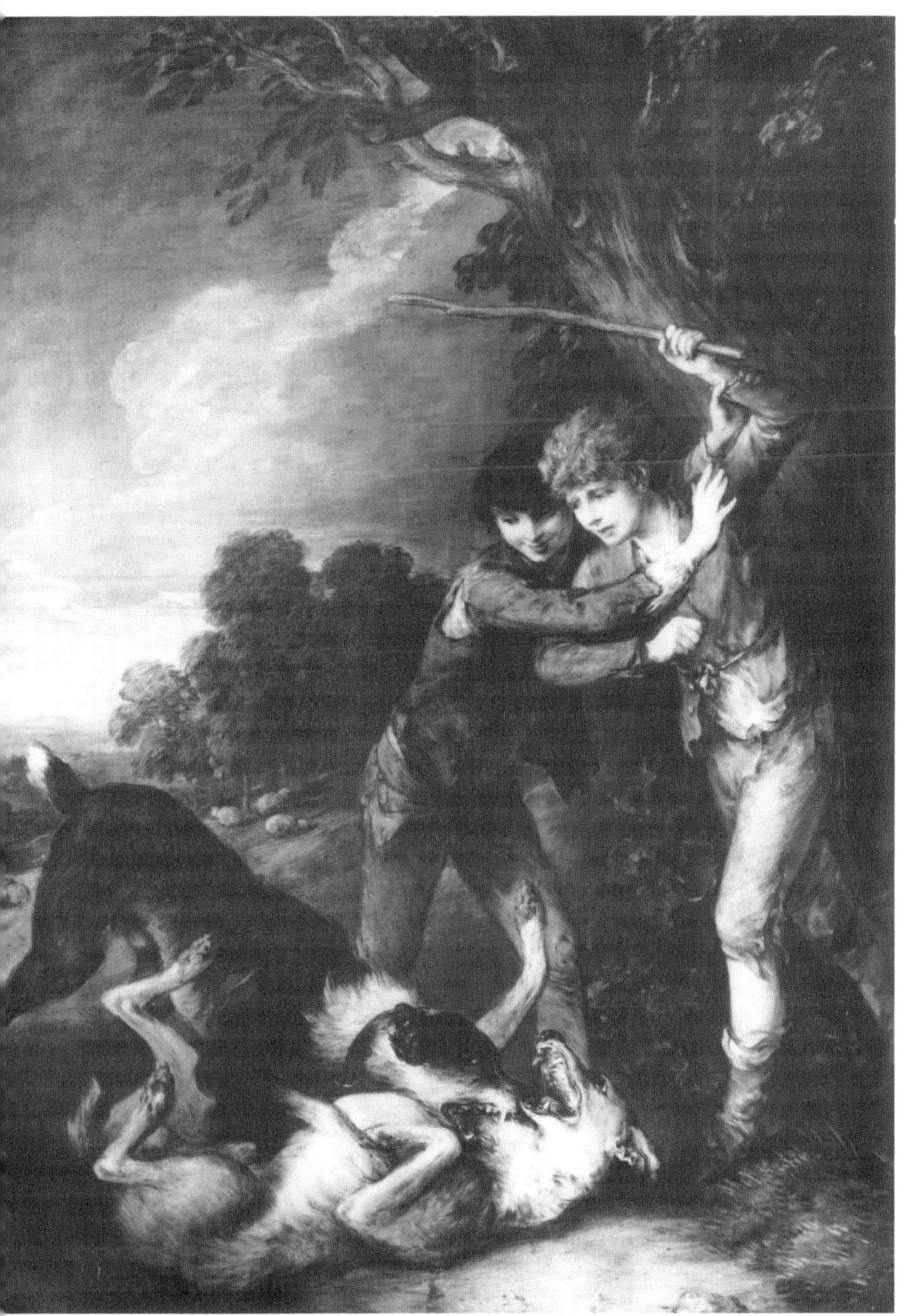

28
THOMAS GAINSBOROUGH, R.A.
Two shepherd boys with dogs fighting, R.A. 1783
oil on canvas, 223.5 × 157.4cm.(88 × 62in.)
Iveagh Bequest, Kenwood, London

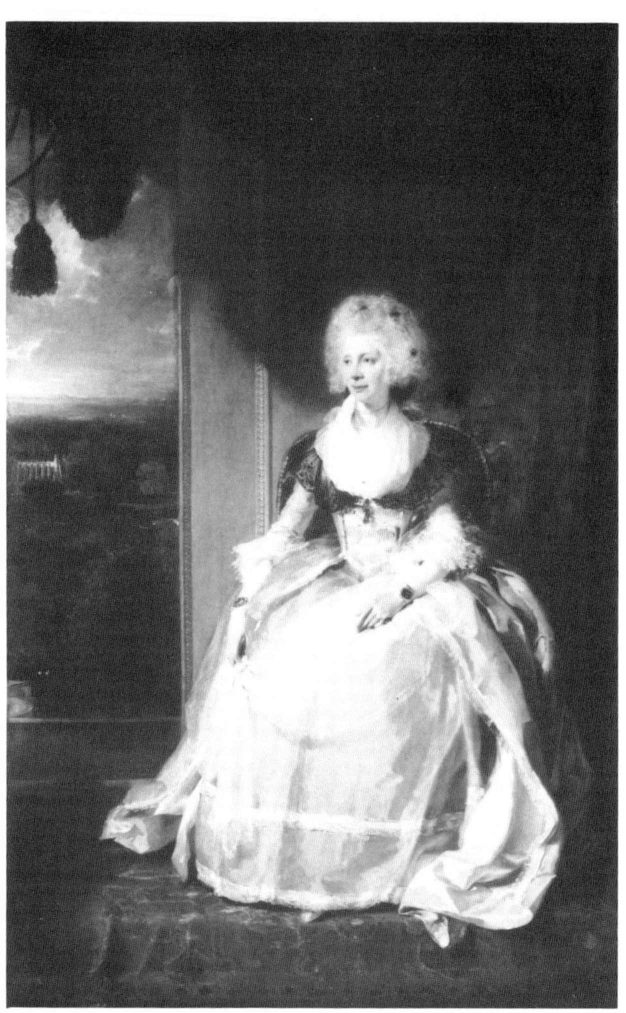

29
SIR THOMAS LAWRENCE, P.R.A.
Queen Charlotte. R.A. 1790
oil on canvas, 239.4 × 147.3cm.(94¼ × 58in.)
National Gallery, London

difficult to see why, for it shows psychological insight coupled with immense virtuosity, qualities that were to stand Lawrence in good stead throughout his career. Lawrence is a marvellous example of how talent can thrive in the right place at the right time. His style matched the sense of style of his subjects; the images he created are inseperable from the Regency he served,

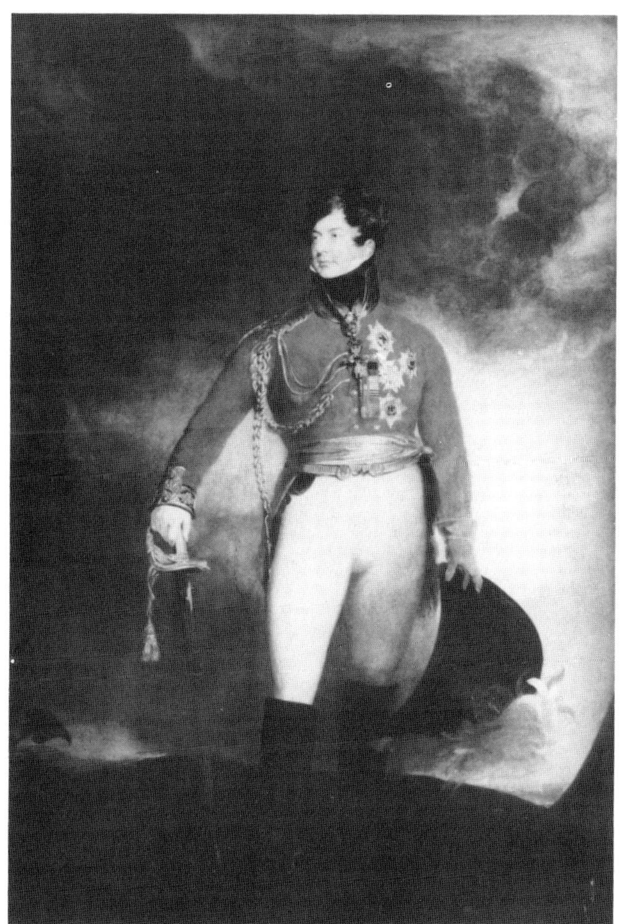

30
SIR THOMAS LAWRENCE, P.R.A.
The Prince Regent, later King George IV, R.A. 1815
oil on canvas, 254 × 152.4cm(100 × 60in.)
Private Collection, U.K.

and the material ostentation of the period finds its full expression in his work. The pursuit of the sheen and brilliance of fine things, and the reflection of a social class infinitely content with itself were translated by Lawrence into pictures of enormous verve and elán (*The Prince Regent, later King George IV,* R.A.1815, Ill.30).

Other fine portraitists who practised during Lawrence's lifetime were Joseph Wright of Derby, Zoffany, Beechey and Raeburn, but the Academy had to wait a long time before it saw a worthy successor to Lawrence. Throughout the nineteenth

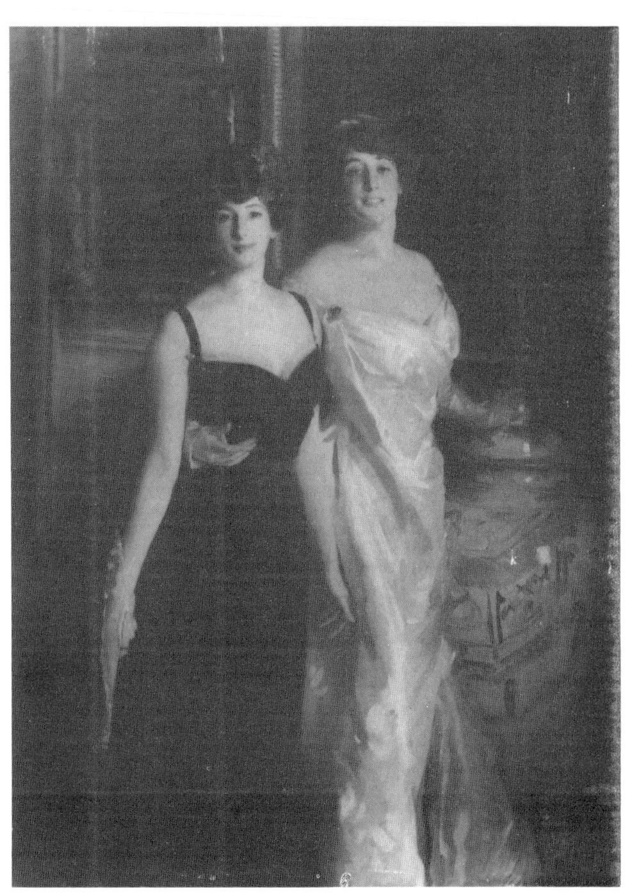

31
JOHN SINGER SARGENT, R.A.
Ena and Betty, Daughters of Asher and Mrs. Wertheimer, R.A. 1901
oil on canvas, 185.5 × 131cm.(73 × 51½in.)
Tate Gallery, London

century thousands of portraits crowded the walls of the annual Exhibitions but most are now happily forgotten in municipal offices and the cellars of museums. Later artists such as Millais or Stevens created some fine portraits as by-products of their usual work but not until John Singer Sargent (Ill. 31) did a portraitist of substantial talent appear at the Academy. Influenced by Manet, Sargent cultivated a bravura style that enjoys some measure of the insight and flair demonstrated earlier by Gainsborough and Lawrence. Other memorable recent portraitists included Orpen (Ill. 61) and Augustus John. Sickert, too, painted some fine

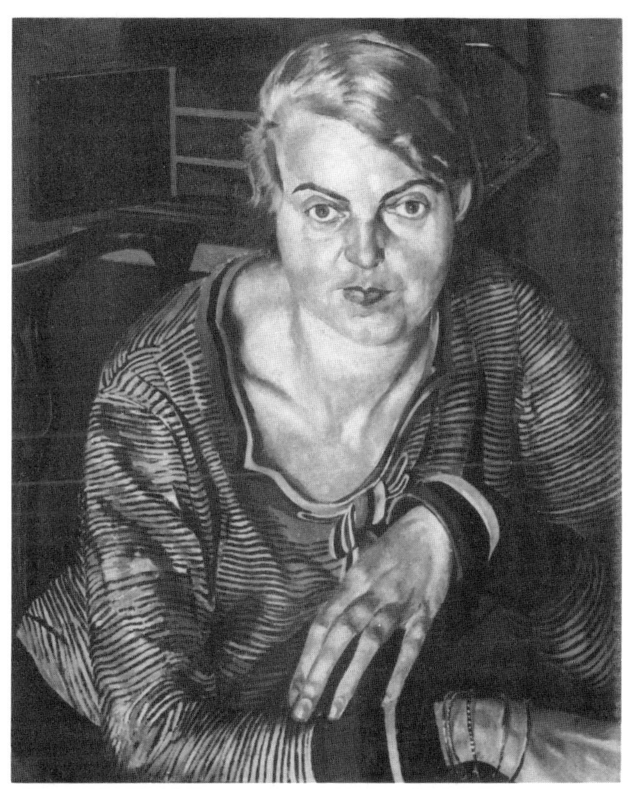

32
STANLEY SPENCER, R.A.
Patricia Preece, R.A. 1934
oil on canvas, 83.9 × 73.6cm.(33 × 29in.)
Southampton Art Gallery
Patricia Preece was Spencer's second wife

portraits and painterliness is also a predominant feature of his work. A different kind of emphasis is evident in Stanley Spencer's *Patricia Preece* (R.A. 1934, Ill. 32). Here we are confronted with a very uncompromising image of twentieth century introspection and alienation. For both Sickert and Spencer the desire to portray mankind was essayed within the larger tradition of aesthetic exploration and fused with an awareness of human psychology, sometimes disturbingly so. Unfortunately these perceptions are sometimes absent from the depictions of prominent personalities that appear in the Royal Academy in our day.

Yet it was neither history painting nor portraiture that was to typify the genius of the Royal Academy in the century after

Reynolds. Instead, it was a branch of art Reynolds considered among the lowest of all that in the event replaced them as the 'glory' of British art.

Landscape

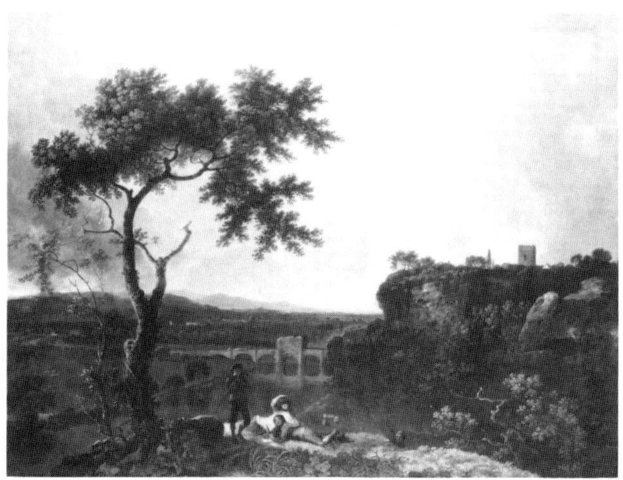

33
RICHARD WILSON, R.A.
Holt Bridge on the River Dee, 1762
oil on canvas, 148.5 × 194.3cm.(58½ × 76½in.)
National Gallery, London
The bridge connects Holt in Wales with Farndon in Cheshire; Farndon church can be seen on the right.

The artist to whom the transformation of this previously limited genre may be credited above any other is Richard Wilson. A founder-Member of the Academy, Wilson subsequently became its Librarian, a post he held until his death in 1782. Although trained as a portraitist, Wilson spent six or seven years in Italy in the 1750s where he was influenced by a great number of landscape painters, including Poussin, Claude and Salvator Rosa.

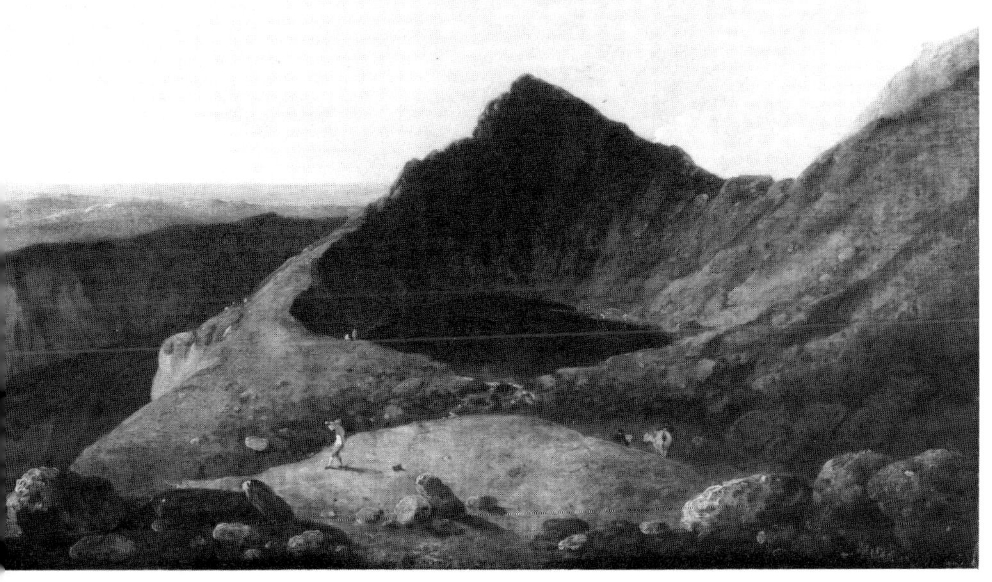

34
RICHARD WILSON, R.A.
Llyn-y-Cau, Cader Idris, R.A. 1774?
oil on canvas, 49.5 × 72.1cm.(19¾ × 28½in.)
Tate Gallery, London

In the years following his return to England he essayed a new type of 'Claudian' landscape, taking as his subject not the invented or 'reconstituted' landscapes of Italy but those of Britain itself. These he treated in the manner of Claude *(Holt Bridge on the River Dee,* 1762, Ill. 33), completely assimilating the principles of that artist's compositions. Like Claude he focused attention on the centre of the picture through the use of a darker periphery and he took care to create a single unifying mood in each picture. Surprisingly, perhaps, the result was not a mannered and lifeless construct of borrowings but a fresh synthesis that deploys a subtle and evocative use of light to communicate deep feeling. In his later paintings Wilson even occasionally allowed his sympathy for his native Wales to overcome his love of the Italianate. *Cader Idris* (R.A. 1774?, Ill. 34) dispenses with Claude altogether and projects the bleak and rugged scenery with great directness.

Gainsborough always took a fundamentally naturalistic

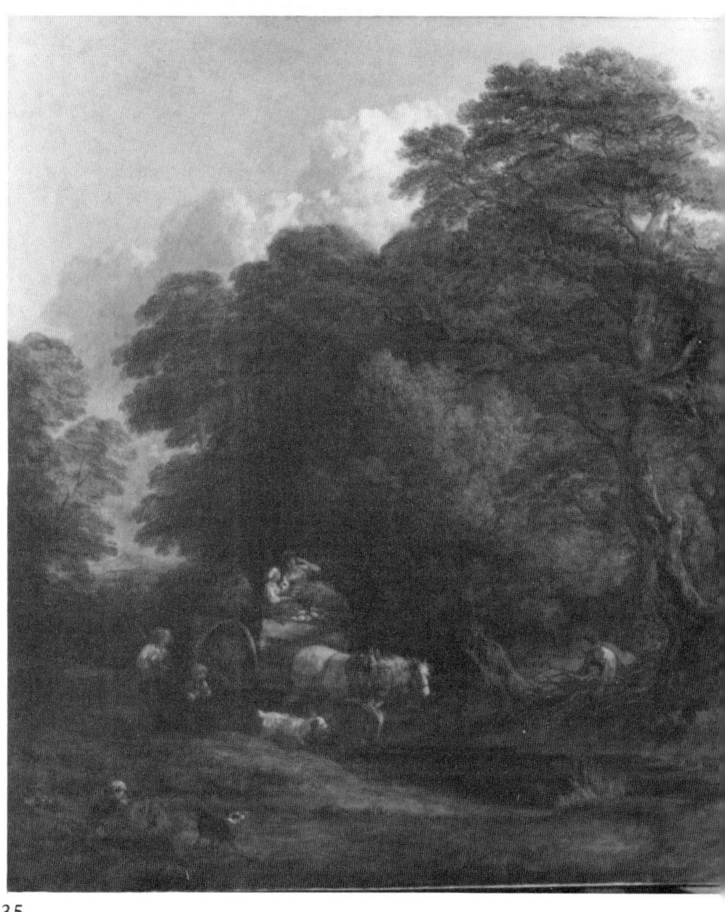

35
THOMAS GAINSBOROUGH, R.A.
The Market Cart, 1786
oil on canvas, 183.5 × 153cm.(72½ × 60¼in.)
Tate Gallery, London

approach to landscape. His love of the subject derived from his early days in Suffolk but unable to find a market for such works he turned towards portraiture to earn a living. Yet his identification with nature never left him and in his greatest pictures in the genre (Ill. 35) he clearly pointed the way towards the type of intimate landscape that Constable was to develop.

A far more dramatic, though equally influential artist, was Philip James De Loutherbourg. Theatricality is the hallmark of his style and it is this artificiality that shows him to be a forerunner of that restlessness of feeling and sense of psychological

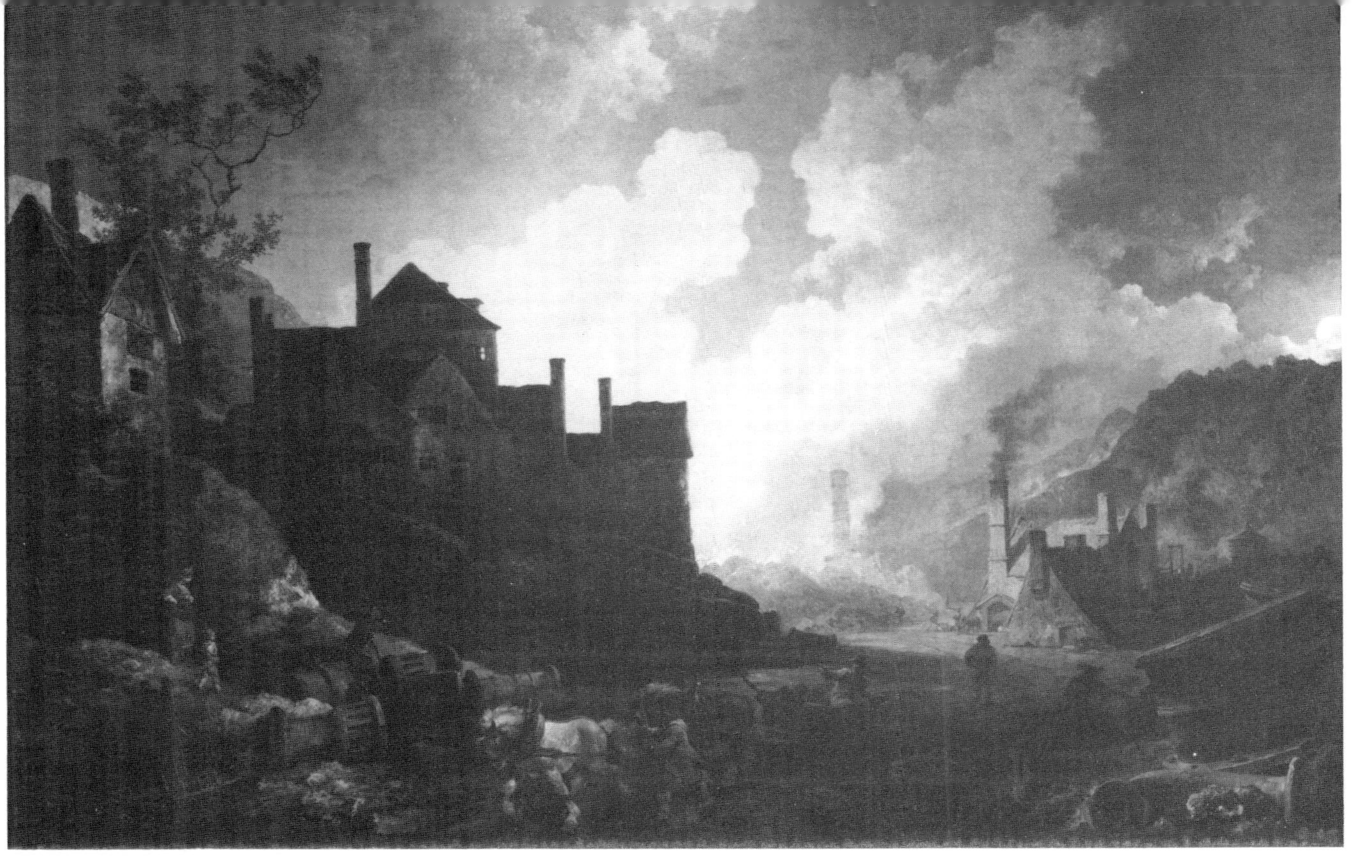

36
PHILIP JAMES DE LOUTHERBOURG, R.A.
Coalbrookdale by Night, R.A. 1801
oil on canvas, 68 × 106.7cm.(26¾ × 42in.)
Science Museum, London

display that has been characterised as Romanticism. De Loutherbourg was born in Hesse-Nassau of French parents and trained in France before coming to England in 1771. Soon afterwards he became the principal scene-painter and stage designer for David Garrick at the Drury Lane Theatre. He was elected an Academician in 1781. His greatest success was his 'Eidophusikon', a primitive *son et lumiere* machine which both undoubtedly heightened his own sense of light and colour and influenced Gainsborough and Turner. De Loutherbourg's dramatic flair was matched by meticulous craftsmanship and the range of his work is large: he painted complex battle scenes, satirical pictures in the tradition of Hogarth and Rowlandson, historical, religious and allegorical paintings as well as straightforward topographical views and intensely dramatic avalanche and snow-scenes. Perhaps his most original single work is his powerful portrayal of the transformation of England by the Industrial Revolution. *A View of Coalbrookdale by Night* (R.A.1801, Ill.36) represents a vision from a contemporary hell. The foreground is lit by the lurid glow of blazing furnaces and projects a sense of complete despoilation. The bare tree up on the extreme left acts both as the key-stone of the pictorial architecture and as a solitary reminder of the pre-industrial landscape. Similarly, the factories and workers in the centre contrast with the farmhouse and farmer's wife and child beneath the tree. Such an appreciation of the ugly cost of industrial progress was often repeated later in the nineteenth century but this painting provides one of the most original, prophetic and disturbing images of its age.

De Loutherbourg's dramatic sense was one of the many influences assimilated by the painter who may be considered the Royal Academy's greatest and most loyal son: Joseph Mallord William Turner. The Royal Academy was at the centre of Turner's artistic and social existence. He studied in the Academy Schools, sat on its councils, participated in its picture-hangings, was for many years the Professor of Perspective and even acted for a short time as substitute President. Characteristically he always chose it as the venue for his most commanding statements. His commitment to the institution was total and his long life matched the period of its greatest contribution to British art.

Few other artists in the history of western painting demonstrate such an enormous progression from their early to their later work as Turner. If we compare the first oil-painting he

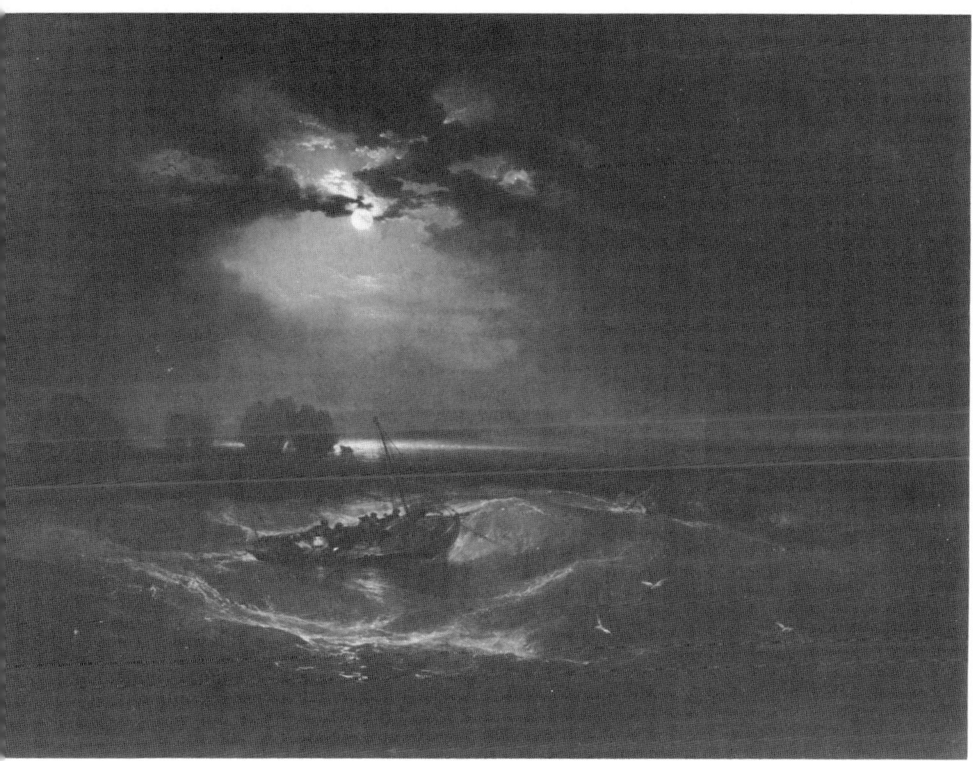

37
J.M.W. TURNER, R.A.
Fishermen at Sea, R.A. 1796
oil on canvas, 91.5 × 122.4cm.(36 × 48½in.)
Tate Gallery, London

exhibited at the Royal Academy, the *Fishermen at Sea* of 1796 (Ill. 37), with one of the last group of works he displayed in 1850 (Ill. 41) it is hard to believe they were created by the same painter. Whereas the early picture is dark and mysterious and rooted in the picturesque values of the eighteenth century, the later work is filled with the most brilliant light and subtle forms in a fusion that verges on the abstract.

Turner was born in London in 1775, the son of a wig-maker and barber. He displayed signs of talent at an early age and was admitted to the Royal Academy Schools at the age of 14. Soon he was regularly exhibiting oil-paintings at the Academy and their extraordinary quality was quickly recognised. He was elected an Associate Academician in 1799 and a full Academician in 1802. In that same year he travelled to France and Switzerland for the

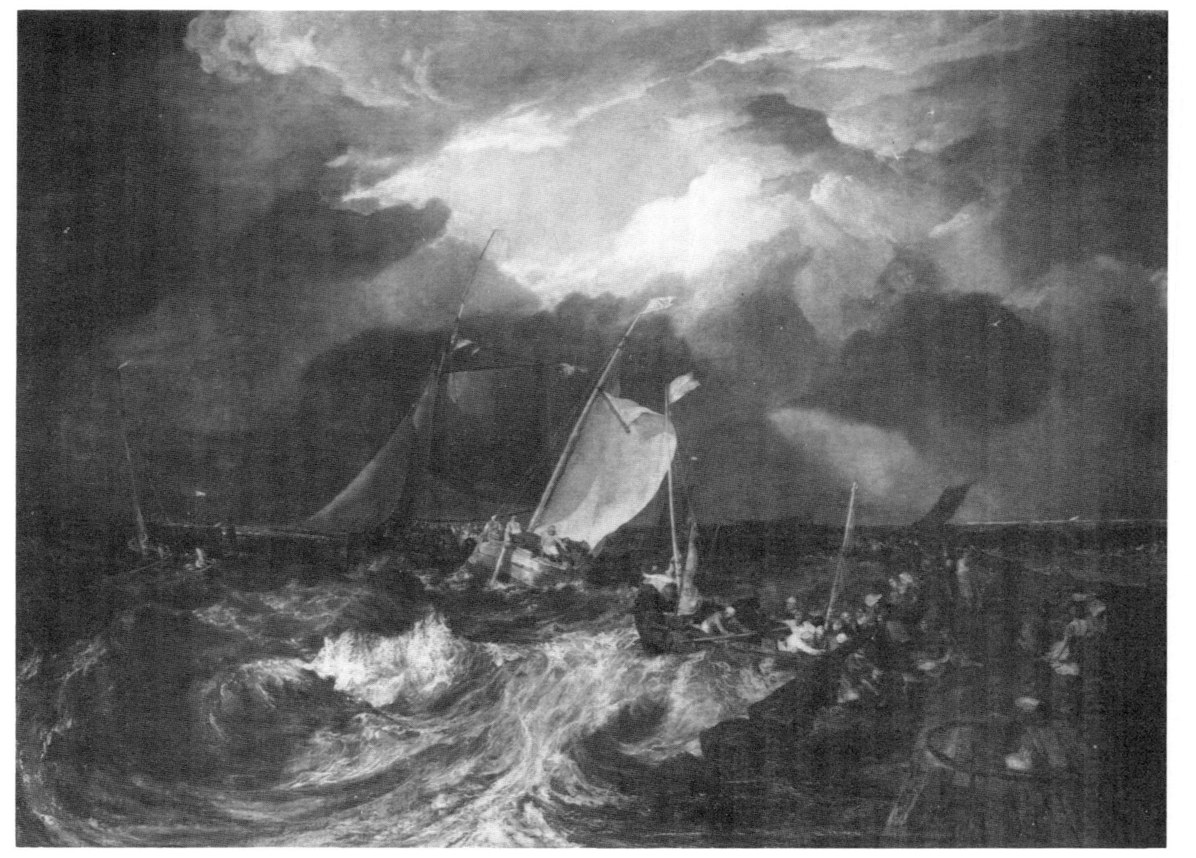

38
J.M.W. TURNER, R.A.
Calais Pier, with French Poissards Preparing for Sea; an English Packet arriving, R.A. 1803
oil on canvas, 172 × 240cm.(67¾ × 94½in.)

first time and he drew on those Continental experiences for work for the Academy. *Calais Pier, with French Poissards Preparing for Sea; an English Packet arriving* (R.A.1803,Ill.38) depicts the stormy scene that Turner witnessed upon first landing in France. At the left of centre we see the channel packet approaching, its passengers drenched and probably seasick. The packet is in danger of colliding with a French fishing-smack, desperately trying to turn away. Equally frantic are the attempts of a small ketch to avoid being smashed against the pier. The swirl of the sea and the black sky are enormously effective and the picture went a long way towards satisfying the contemporary taste for 'sublime' (i.e. fearful) experience – much like watching a 'disaster film' today.

In 1812 Turner exhibited his *Snow Storm: Hannibal and his Army crossing the Alps* (Ill.14). The work was accompanied in the Royal Academy catalogue by an extract from a 'poem' by Turner pondering the dangers of victory. We see the Carthaginian army as it descends into Italy, preyed upon by fierce mountain-tribesmen. Eventually, the poem tells us, this army would dissipate its strength idling upon 'Capua's joys'. It was an apposite theme. When Turner painted *Hannibal*, Napoleon was rampaging through Europe and the artist doubtless intended the picture to act as a direct reminder that such empire-building always contains the seeds of its own destruction. As it had been with Hannibal, so it would be with Napoleon, power-mania, avarice and the need for luxury inevitably leading to decline and fall. This theme was to recur in a number of Turner's important later works made when the British Empire was at its apogee. In them Turner cited the examples of other failed empires, such as Rome and Venice, to further point the moral.

By 1815 Turner was at the height of his powers. That year he exhibited *Dido building Carthage: or the rise of the Carthaginian Empire* (Plate III), the work he considered his 'chef d'oeuvre'. He always refused to sell it and eventually even requested that he should be buried rolled up in it, though thankfully he was dissuaded from carrying out this intention. The picture is a superbly-structured elaboration of its subject. On the left Dido is overseeing the building of Carthage, surrounded by architects, surveyors and masons. At the opposite side of the picture is the tomb of Dido's dead husband, Sychaeus, who had been murdered by her brother. She had fled from Tyre with Sychaeus's

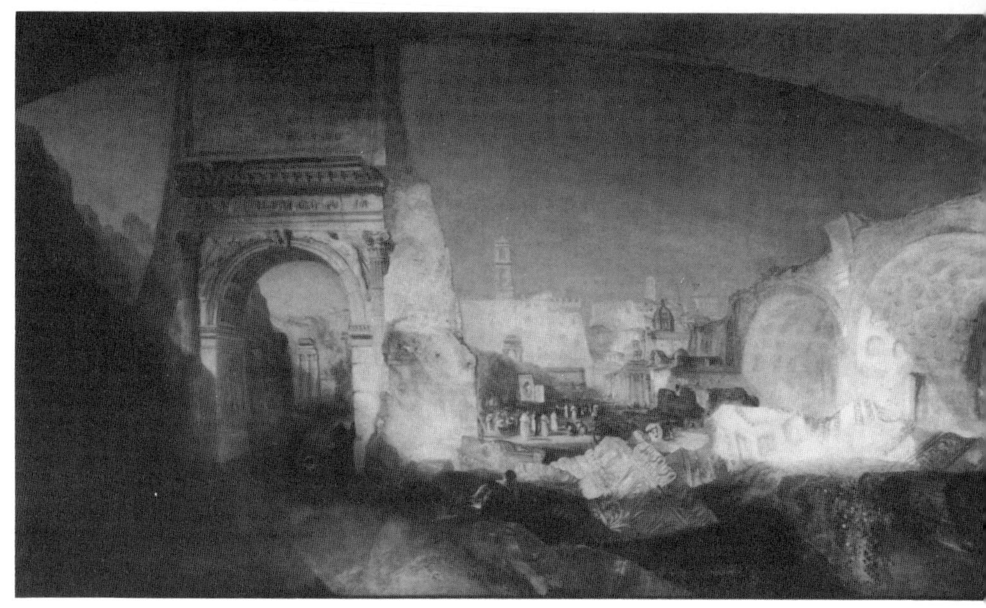

39
J.M.W. TURNER, R.A.
Forum Romanum, for Mr. Soane's Museum, R.A. 1826
oil on canvas, 145.5 × 237.5cm.(57½ × 93in.)
Tate Gallery, London
Turner painted this for Sir John Soane but it was not to Soane's taste and he exchanged it for another painting by Turner.

remains to found a new city on the shores of North Africa. Turner purposefully contrasts the forces of life, on the left, with a reminder of man's ultimate fate, on the right. On the left some small boys are sailing toy boats, and the distant ship-building works, the state barge and the sunrise clearly all additionally allude to the future rise of Carthage to Mediterranean naval supremacy. The newly-building city also suggests the larger concept of building the peace, a relevant issue in 1814-15 at the end of the Napoleonic Wars.

Turner travelled much during these years and in 1819 he went to Italy for the first time, visiting Rome and Venice and making over two thousand sketches of Italian scenery alone. On his return he painted some large-scale Italian views, including the *Forum Romanum* (R.A. 1826, Ill. 39), but not until the 1830s did he turn his attention seriously to Venice.

Turner rarely missed exhibiting annually at the Academy. In 1838-39 he painted what is often considered to be his master-

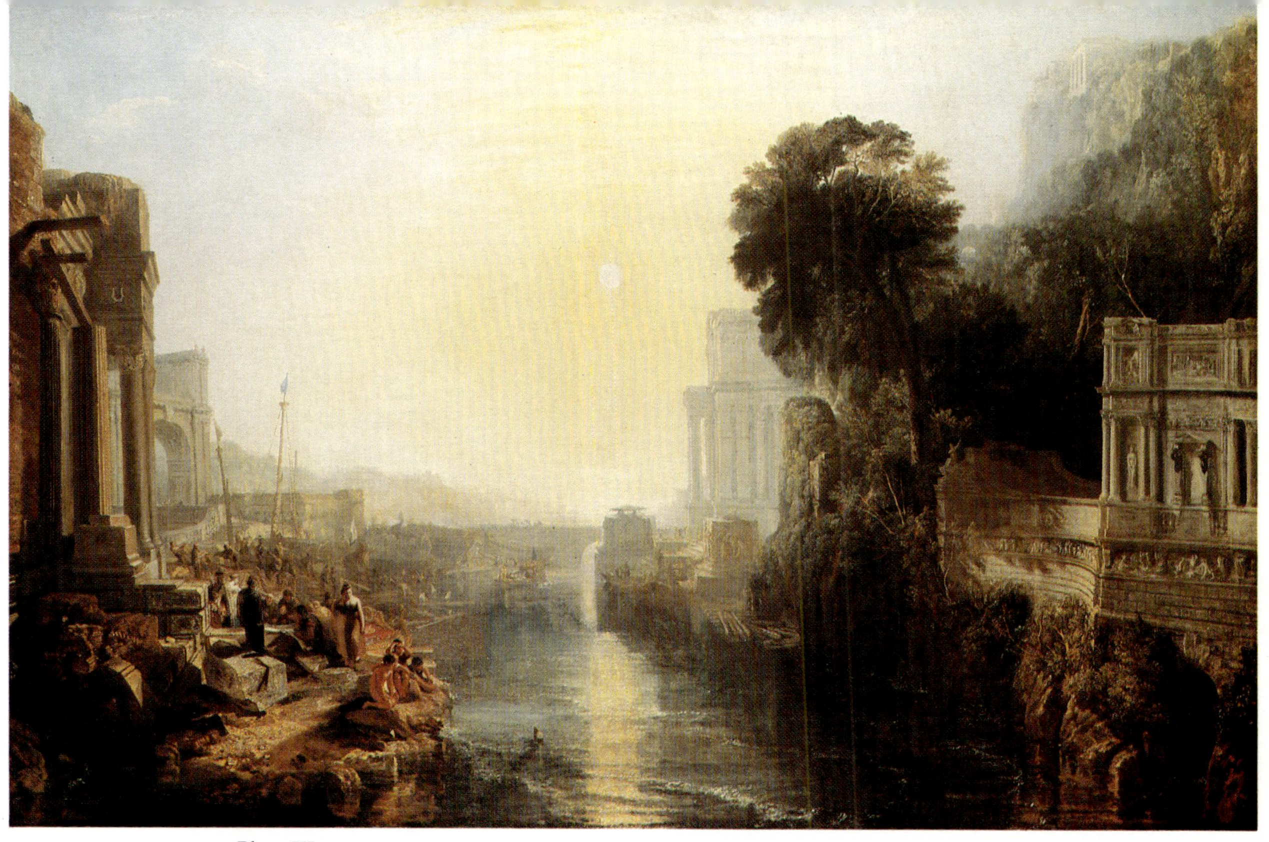

Plate III
J.M.W. TURNER, R.A.
Dido building Carthage; or the Rise of the Carthaginian Empire R.A. 1815
oil on canvas, 155.5 × 232cm.(61¼ × 91¼in.)
National Gallery, London

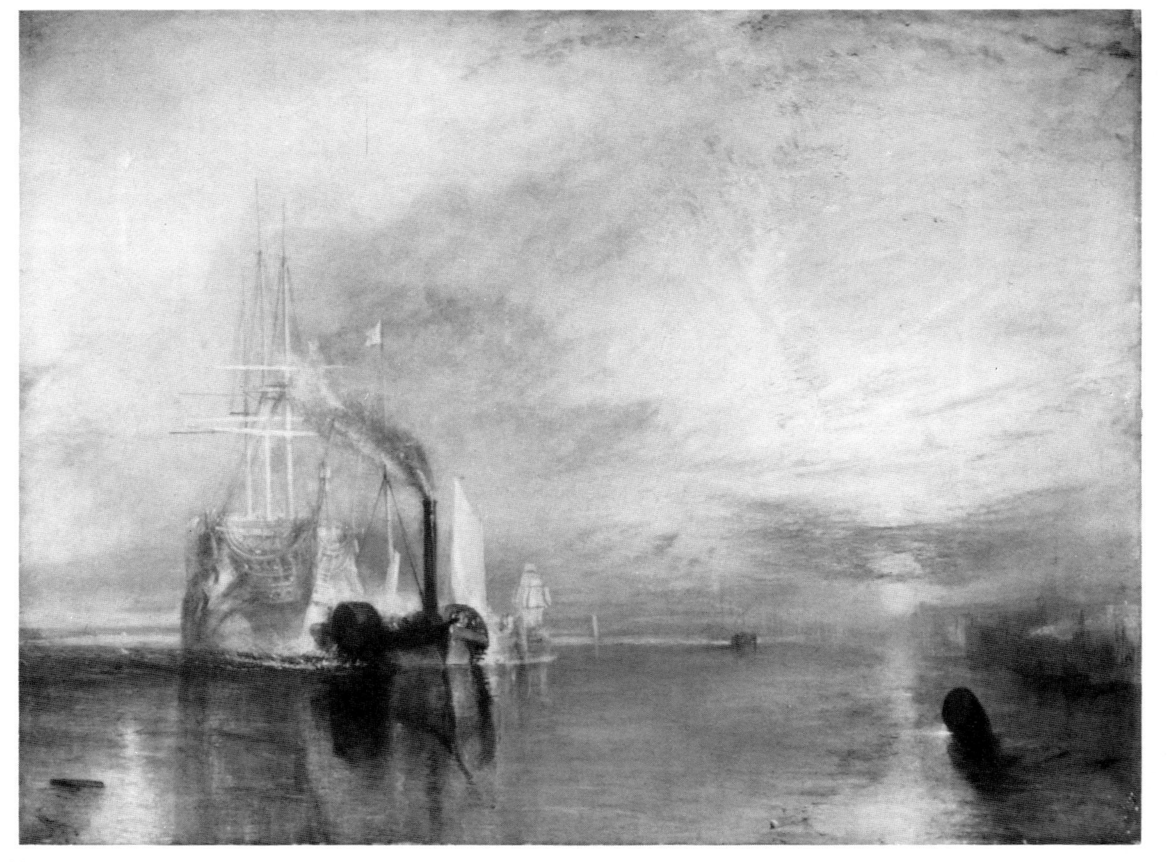

40

J.M.W. TURNER, R.A.

The Fighting 'Temeraire', tugged to her Last Berth to be broken up, 1838, R.A. 1839

oil on canvas, 91 × 122cm (35¼ × 48in.)

piece, *The Fighting 'Temeraire', tugged to her Last Berth to be broken up, 1838* (R.A. 1839, Ill. 40). This work needs little analysis. It has always spoken clearly of the replacement of the age of sail by the more sombre values of industrialised power. Turner intentionally places the steam-tug's funnel in front of its mast to symbolise the coming of Steam to the fore in naval matters and, by contrast with the tug's black colour and squat form, the vast man-of-war glides like a ghost ship across the water, its masts and rigging dressed in full order as they might have appeared forty years before when it was a ship of the line.

Turner continued painting right up until the end of his life. His works eventually totalled some five hundred and fifty oils and nearly two thousand water-colours, a record of productivity that is truly astounding. In 1850, in his mid-seventies, he made one last supreme effort and sent four paintings to the Academy, all on the theme of Dido and Aeneas (Ill. 41). It was a very apt subject. Virgil's Dido had been abandoned by Aeneas because he had a greater destiny: to found Rome. Dido symbolised everything that Turner had sacrificed. Like Aeneas, he too had abandoned the possibility of a settled, comfortable existence, the enjoyment of wealth and secure family relationships, all for a higher calling. The result was one of the finest achievements in western art.

Whereas Turner's taste was for the visionary use of landscape as a dramatic setting for the human comedy, for Constable the natural world served as the entire content of his art. Ruskin missed the point entirely when he stated that

> Constable perceives in a landscape that the grass is wet, the meadows flat and the boughs shady; that is to say, about as much as, I suppose, might in general be apprehended, between them, by an intelligent fawn and a skylark.

It is precisely this awareness of the unassuming character of nature that gives Constable's finest painting its immediacy and lyricism. When Constable began to paint the world as he perceived it, rather than as it was seen through the artistic conventions of the time, his attitude to nature was completely new. To find nature in itself an adequate subject for art was Constable's greatest innovation. He tried to approach it without preconceptions, and he allowed it to determine the responses

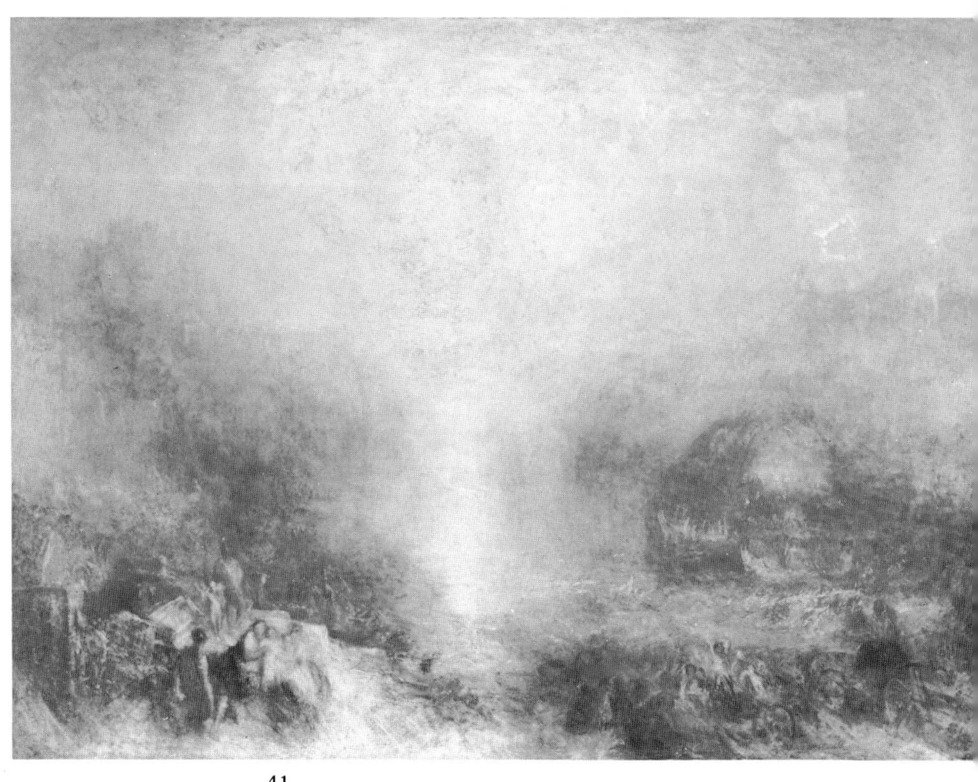

41
J.M.W. TURNER, R.A.
Mercury sent to admonish Aeneas, R.A. 1850
oil on canvas, 90.5 × 121cm.(35½ × 47½in.)
Tate Gallery, London
The painting was exhibited with the following verses by Turner:

Beneath the morning mist,
Mercury waited to tell him of his neglected fleet
Ms. *Fallacies of Hope*

Mercury was sent to remind Aeneas of his destiny to leave Carthage and found Rome. Turner seems to have depicted the scene a moment after Mercury had delivered the message and vanished into thin air.

capable of expressing its changing moods. The result is an art that is fresh, lyrical and spontaneous. It is profoundly evocative and ever more relevant in a world increasingly spoilt by man.

Constable was born in East Bergholt, Suffolk, the son of a miller. The local landscape formed him. The relatively flat and unspectacular Suffolk countryside caused him to look intensely at

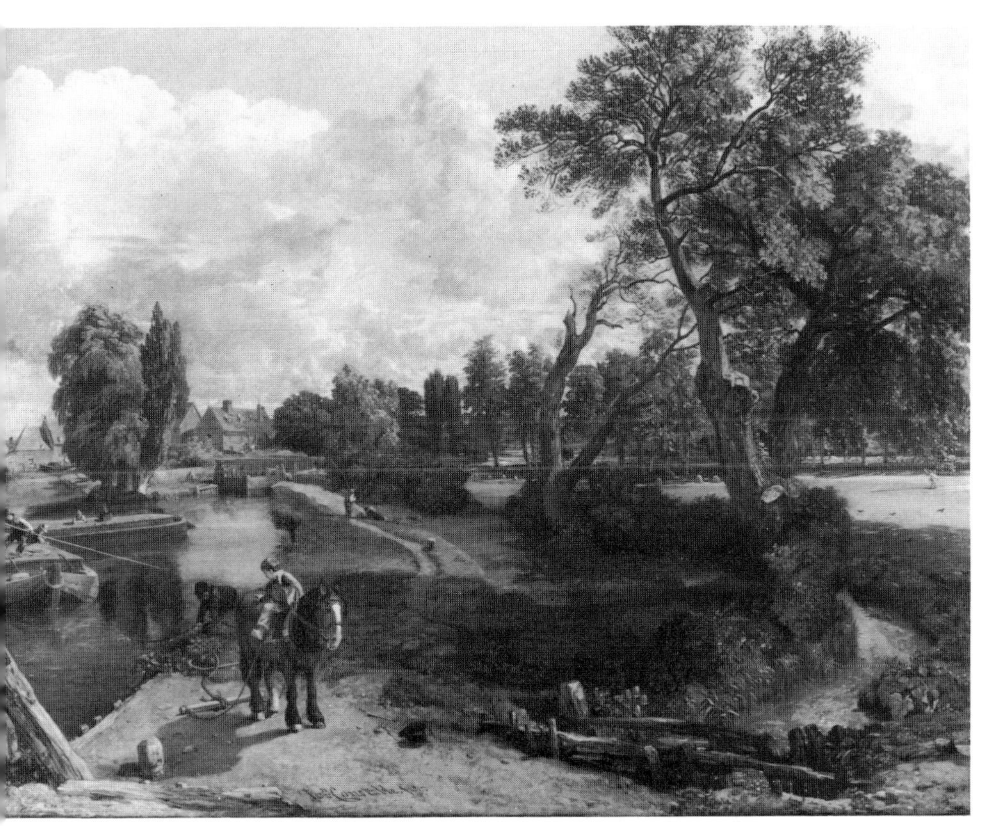

42
JOHN CONSTABLE, R.A.
Scene on a navigable river (Flatford Mill), R.A. 1817
oil on canvas, 101.7 X 127cm.(40 × 50in.)
Tate Gallery, London

aspects of his surroundings that were usually taken for granted:

> the sound of water escaping from Mill dams... Willows, old rotten Banks, slimy posts and brickwork. I love such things ... As long as I do paint I shall never cease to paint such places. They have always been my delight.

In 1799 he enrolled at the Royal Academy Schools and three years later exhibited for the first time at the Academy. Soon afterwards he returned to Suffolk and supported himself by portrait and religious commissions. Gradually he turned to landscape.

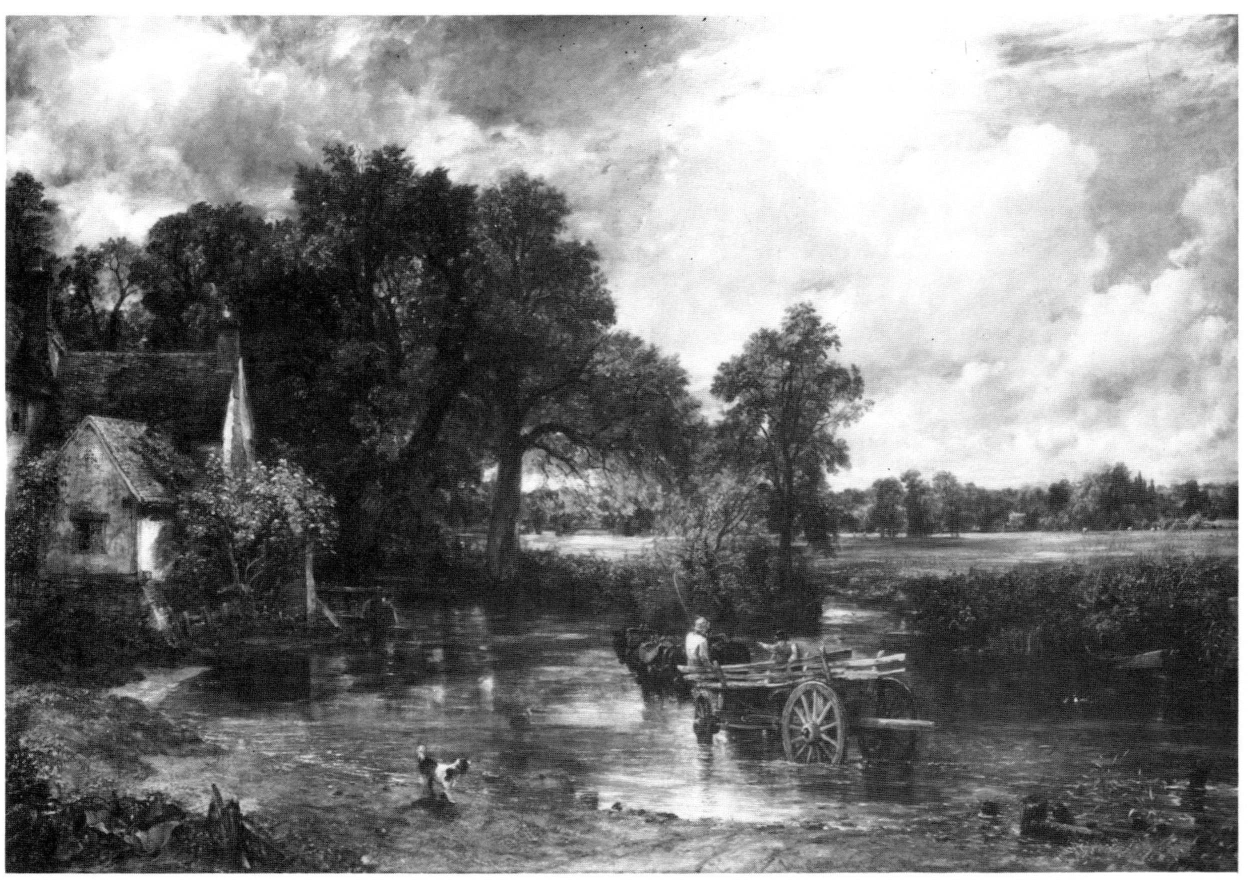

43
JOHN CONSTABLE, R.A.
Landscape:Noon (The Hay-Wain), R.A. 1821
oil on canvas, 130.5 × 185.5cm.(51¼ × 73in.)

Not until the end of the 1810s, however, did he produce the masterpieces by which he is best known. These include *Flatford Mill* (R.A. 1817, Ill. 42), *Dedham Lock and Mill* (R.A. 1819), *Stratford Mill* (R.A. 1820), *The Hay-Wain* (R.A. 1821, Ill. 43) and the great *Salisbury Cathedral* of 1823. They embody the essence of English landscape, its freshness, fertility and tranquillity, and they express the harmony of man and nature with quiet simplicity.

Constable had a great struggle to win acceptance at the Royal Academy, and was not elected an Associate until 1819. Only after many successive rejections was he finally elevated to the status of Academician in 1829, by which time he was somewhat embittered by his struggle for recognition at the Academy. His evident relief at election is expressed in the title of his Diploma work – *A Boat passing a Lock* (Ill. 60).

In the meantime, however, he had found patrons for his work and in 1824 won a Gold Medal at the Paris Salon for three paintings, among them *The Hay-Wain.* The pictures greatly impressed French artists, especially Delacroix, who repainted a passage in his *Massacre at Chios* as a result. In the 1829 Academy exhibition Constable exhibited *The Cornfield* (Plate IV), a work which is infused with gentle nostalgia for the scenes of his childhood. The picture depicts the lane and path leading from East Bergholt across the fields to Dedham, the route that Constable had used to walk to school as a boy (though the church in the distance was added to the painting to improve the composition).

Towards the end of his career, from the late 1820's onwards, a change came over Constable's work. His practise of working up pictures in the studio from sketches and oil-studies continued but a new artificiality began to creep in. The paint is handled with greater expressiveness and symbolism begins to appear in the works. This change may have been induced partly by the influence of Turner and partly by a feeling that his simple unquestioning response to nature was no longer adequate in the increasingly lonely and hostile world in which he felt he was living (his wife had died in 1828 and these were the years of Reform agitation). This melancholic mood is clearly expressed in the *Cenotaph* (Ill. 44) which occupied him between 1833 and 1836. The picture depicts a monument to the memory of Sir Joshua Reynolds which had been erected by Sir George Beaumont, an early patron of Constable. On either side of the

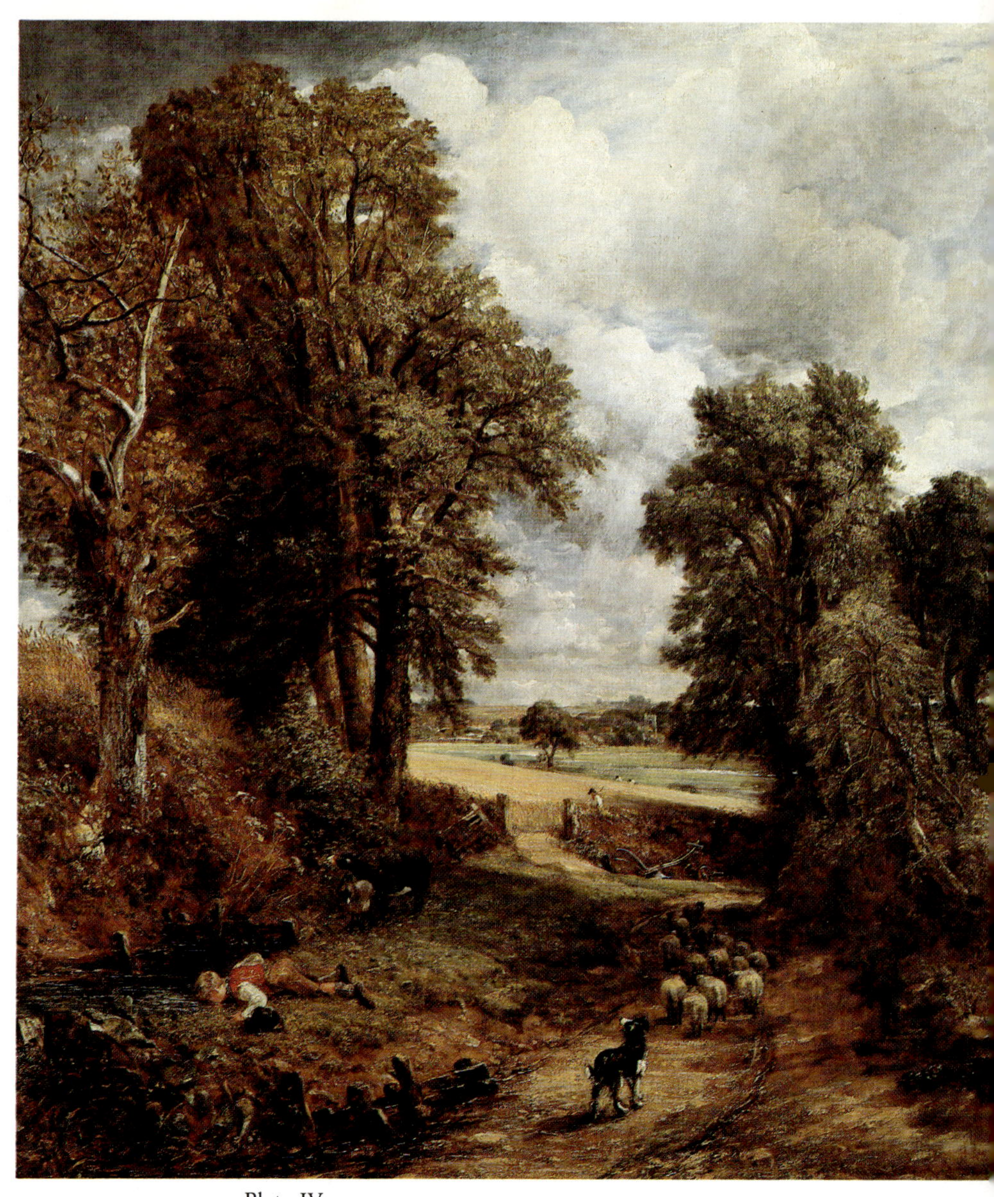

Plate IV
JOHN CONSTABLE, R.A.
Landscape (The Cornfield)
R.A. 1826
oil on canvas, 143 × 122cm.(56¼ × 48in.)
National Gallery, London

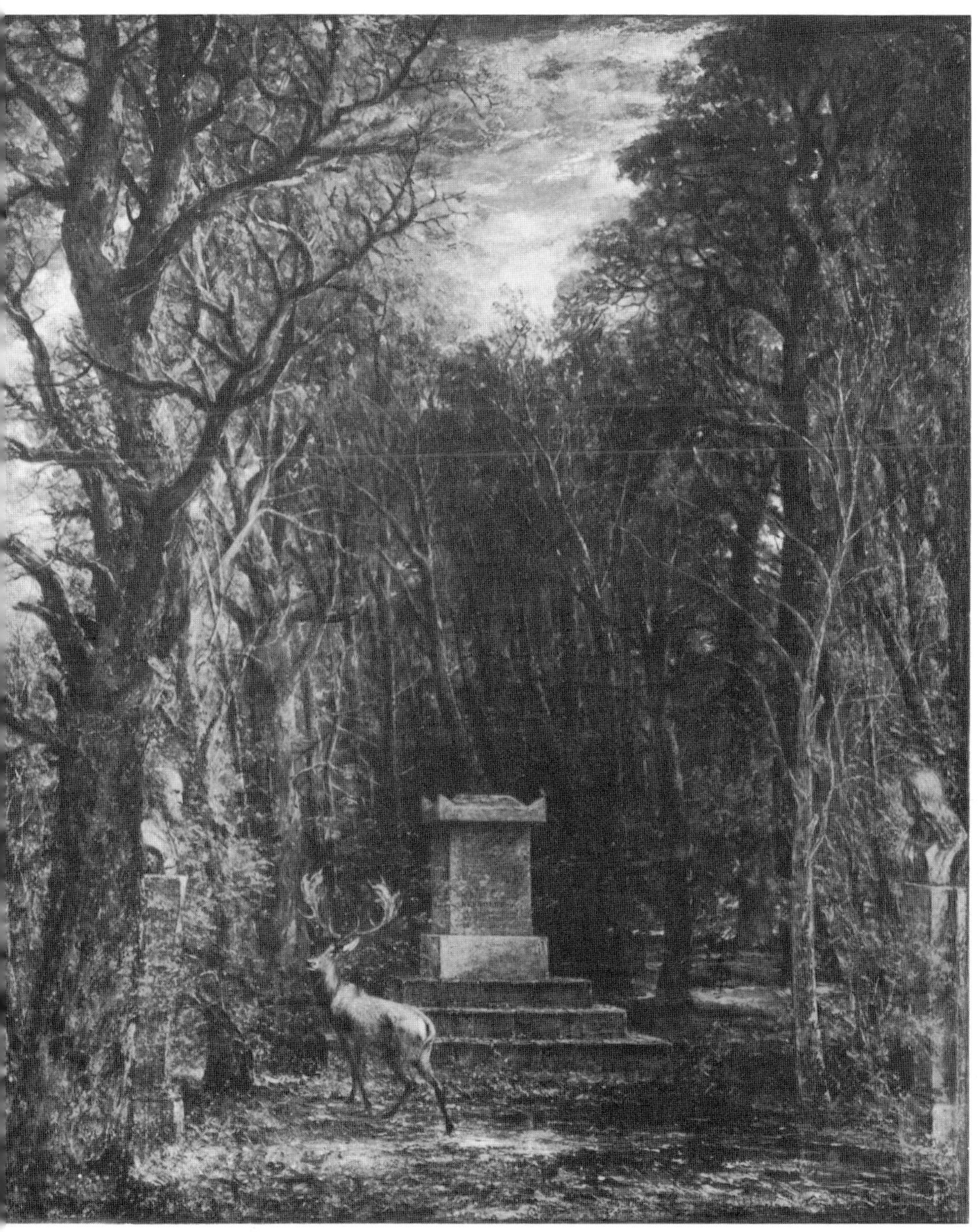

44
JOHN CONSTABLE, R.A.
Cenotaph to the memory of Sir Joshua Reynolds,
rected in the grounds of Corleorton Hall, Leicestershire,
by the late Sir George Beaumont, Bart., R.A. 1836
oil on canvas, 132 × 108.5cm.(52 × 42¾in.)
National Gallery, London

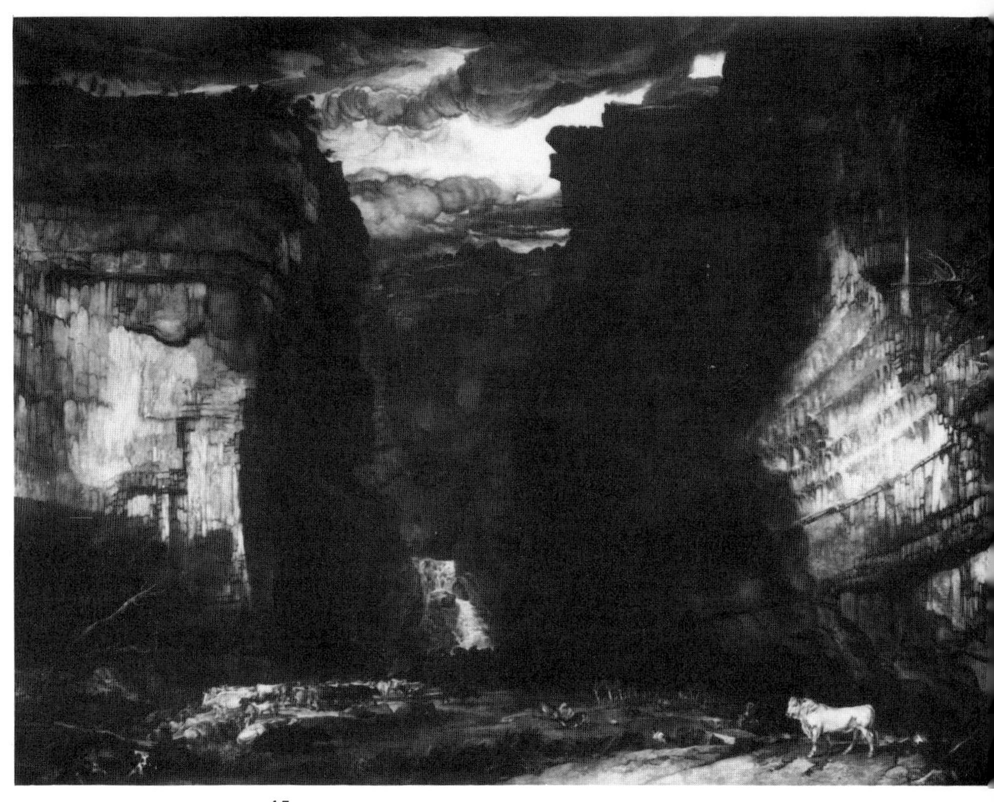

45
JAMES WARD, R.A.
Gordale Scar, 1811-15, R.A. 1815
oil on canvas, 332.7 × 421.6cm.(131 × 166in.)
Tate Gallery, London

memorial are busts of Michelangelo and Raphael, two of Reynolds' great inspirations. The work is elegaic and desolate and it was the last completed painting that Constable exhibited at the Royal Academy. Fittingly, it was displayed in the final exhibition held by the Academy in Somerset House in 1836. Constable showed it in preference to another painting because he '... preferred to see Sir Joshua Reynolds' name ... once more in the catalogue, for the last time in the old house.'

Constable did not live to see the Academy move into its new premises in 1837. His death at the age of 61 robbed British art of a major talent. His output was not as extensive nor as varied in content and form as Turner's but of the two he was undoubtedly the more influential. It is not difficult to see the roots of

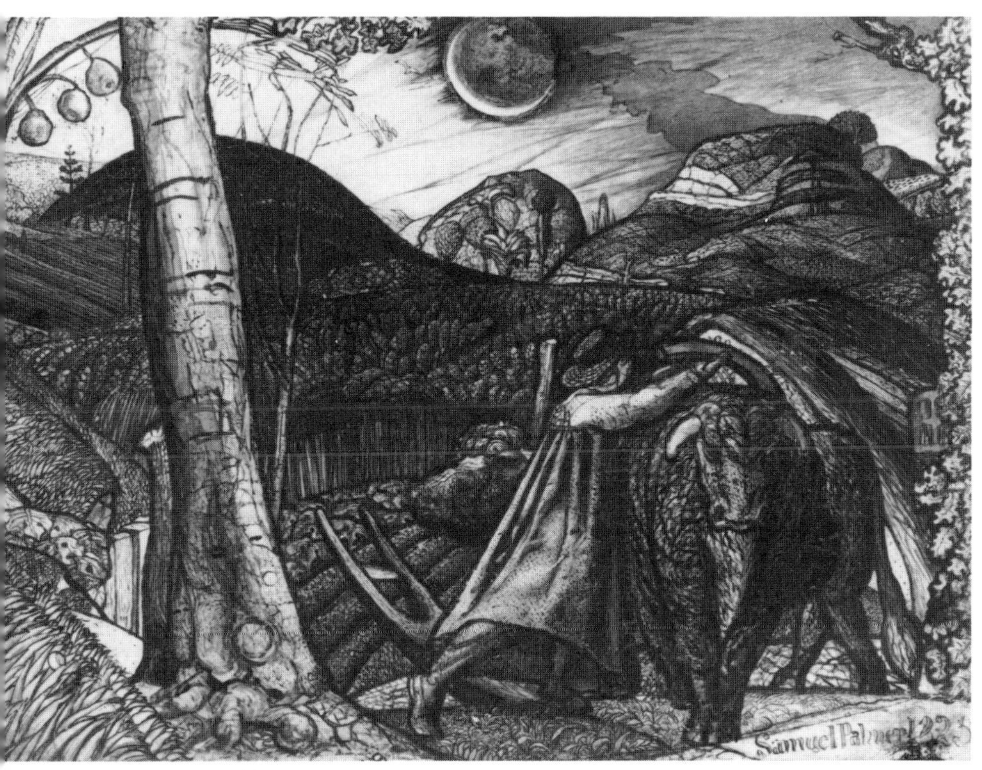

46
SAMUEL PALMER
A Rustic Scene, 1825, R.A. 1826
sepia mixed with gum on paper and varnished
17.5 × 23.6cm.(7 × 9¼in.)
Ashmolean Museum, Oxford

Impressionism as lying partly in Constable's art, most particularly in his oil-studies. Constable's life was a long uphill struggle to justify the self-sufficient experiencing of nature as a fit subject for painting. It is a testament to his genius that we now take that sufficiency for granted.

A great number of other landscape and marine artists have been active in the Academy. Their efforts stretch from the sublime (Ill.45) to the ridiculous, from the visionary (Ill. 46) to the prosaic. The practise of landscape painting has, of course, continued in England to this day. Other fine landscapists and marine artists who were either Academicians or who frequently showed in the Academy were Paul Sandby, Clarkson Stanfield, Augustus Wall Callcott, Edward William Cook, Henry Moore,

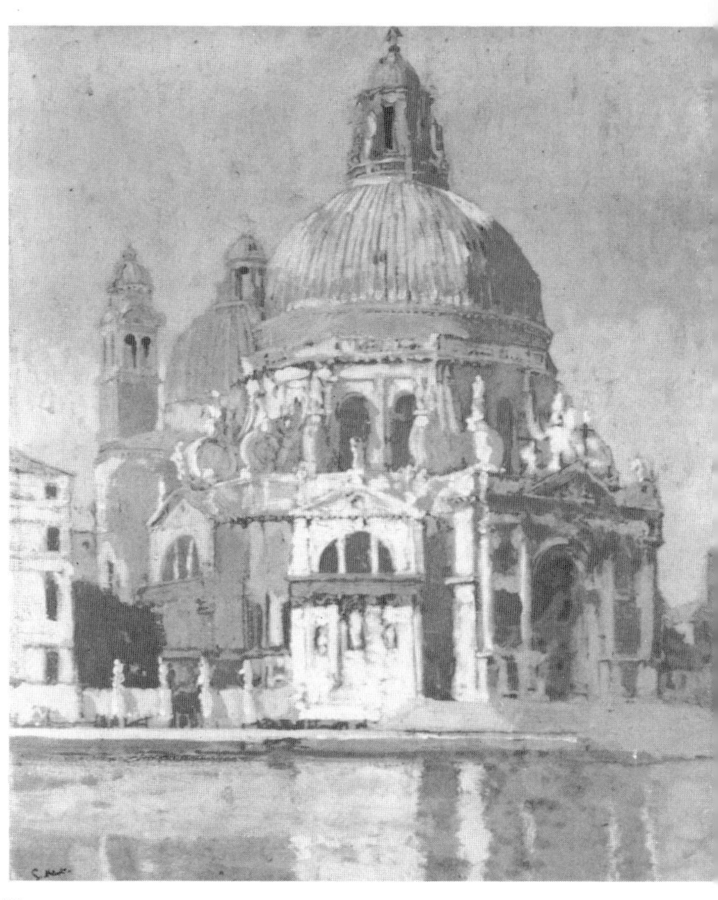

47
WALTER SICKERT, R.A.
*Santa Maria Della Salute, Venice, c.*1901
R.A. Diploma Work 1935
oil on canvas, 55.8 × 45.7cm.(22 × 18in.)
Royal Academy of Arts, London

John Brett, Philip Wilson Steer, John Nash, Walter Sickert (Ill. 47), Stanley Spencer and L.S. Lowry.

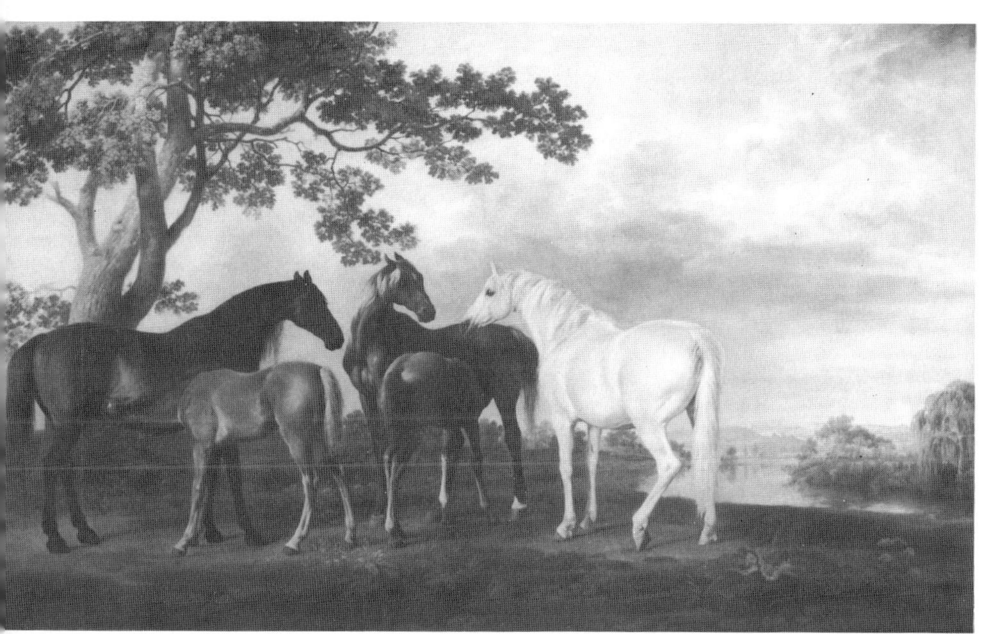

48
GEORGE STUBBS, A.R.A.
*Mares and foals in a river landscape, c.*1763-8
oil on canvas, 99 × 158cm.(39 × 62½in.)
Tate Gallery, London

Animal Painting

Another genre frequently encountered on the walls of the Royal Academy was the painting of animals, and horses in particular. Its greatest practitioner was undoubtedly George Stubbs, although, like Joseph of Wright of Derby before him, he refused to become an Academician, in his case declining (for some unknown reason) to deposit the necessary Diploma work.

It is perhaps misleading to categorise Stubbs merely as an animal artist. He was also a painter of excellent portraits, landscapes, open-air conversation pieces and magnificent hunting-scenes. However, it was his extensive training and practise as an equestrian artist that led to his fame and such subjects always

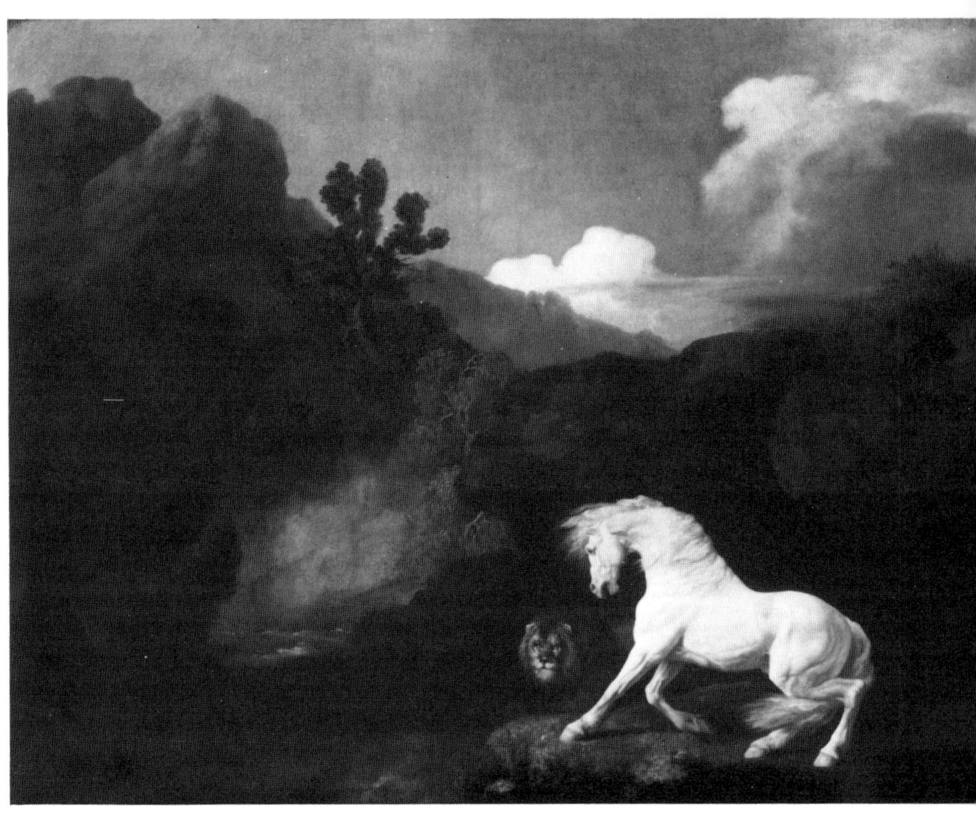

49
GEORGE STUBBS, A.R.A.
Horse frightened by a lion, 1770
oil on canvas, 101.6 × 127cm.(40 × 50in.)
Walker Art Gallery, Liverpool

formed the centre of his artistic endeavours. His engraved work *The Anatomy of the Horse,* for which he spent four years dissecting and drawing horses, established his reputation throughout Europe, and during a long and varied career he painted a vast number of horses and other animals in every mood from the docile to the frenzied. Stubbs' emotional range is wide and we can see in his painting both a serene classicism, as in *Mares and foals in a river landscape* (1763-68,Ill.48), or the highly charged heroic Romanticism of *Horse frightened by a lion* (1770, Ill. 49). In this picture, one of the most haunting images of late eighteenth century art, the Sublime background of silently mysterious mountain chasms and peaceful clouds acts as a superb foil to the scene of terror and impending violence in the foreground. Stubbs

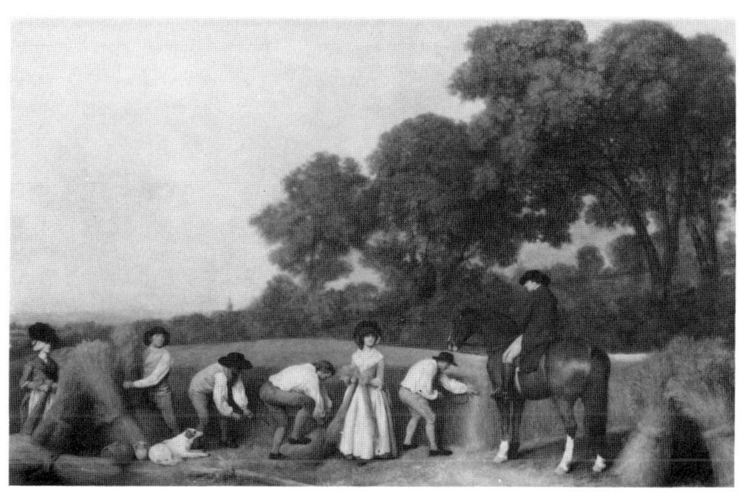

50
GEORGE STUBBS, A.R.A.
Reapers, dated 1784, R.A. 1786
oil on panel, 90.1 × 137.1cm.(35½ × 54in.)
Tate Gallery, London

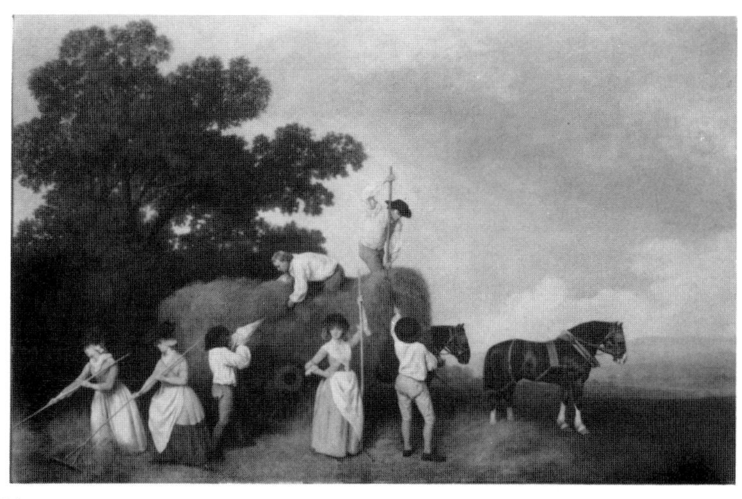

51
GEORGE STUBBS, A.R.A.
Haymakers, dated 1785, R.A. 1786
oil on panel, 90.1 × 137.1cm.(35½ × 54in.)
Tate Gallery,London

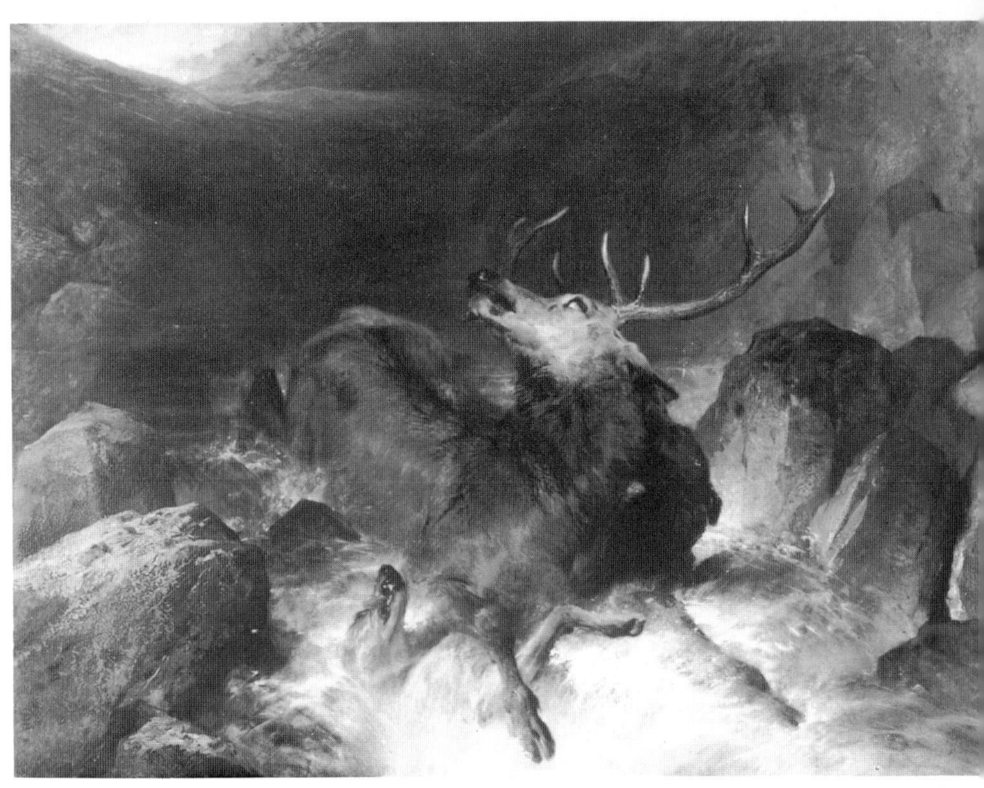

52
SIR EDWIN LANDSEER, R.A.
Deer and Deerhounds in a mountain torrent
R.A. 1833
oil on panel, 70.4 × 90.8cm.(27¾ × 35¾in.)
Tate Gallery, London

always complemented his animals with a landscape setting that would create a suitable unifying mood in his works, and like the later Gainsborough, he understood nature's underlying ferocity. Also like Gainsborough, Stubbs saw the relationship of man to nature as essentially a balanced one. This viewpoint can be seen in his pictures of *Reapers* and *Haymakers* (R.A. 1786, Ills. 50 and 51). Stubbs underpins both works with a rigid linear structure that turns them into a clear statement about the relationship of the rural classes in eighteenth century England.

Among later Academicians there were some extremely proficient animal painters, of whom two are particularly important, James Ward and Edwin Landseer. The latter achieved huge popularity in his day, particularly with Queen Victoria. His animals (*Deer and Deerhounds in a mountain torrent,* R.A.1833, Ill. 52) are clearly invested with human characteristics and emotions which made them potent symbols for the Victorians, though today many of them may seem nauseatingly sentimental. The tradition of animal painting has also been apparent in the Academy down to our time, notably in the works of Alfred Munnings, a recent President of the institution.

Genre Painting

The term 'genre' can simply mean type of subject-matter but more usually it has been used to describe scenes of everyday life, particularly at humble levels. Gainsborough, impressed by Dutch Genre painting, had a great influence on the development of the tradition. There was by his time a tendency for the wealthy to hanker for lowly simplicities (as long as they stayed on the walls) which engendered a demand for such art. The paintings of George Morland, in particular, were enormously popular (he is reputed to have painted more than four thousand) and they fix for ever the popular image of late eighteenth century pastoralism, a benign world seemingly untroubled and endearingly naive *(Inside of a stable,* R.A. 1791, Ill. 53).

The greatest exponent of Genre was David Wilkie. Under the influence of Teniers, Rembrandt, Ostade and Hogarth, Wilkie developed a considerable technique and his debut picture at the Royal Academy, *The Village Politicians* (R.A. 1806, Ill. 54) created a sensation, although it appears today as an embarrassing piece of condescension, representing the peasantry as virtual idiots. Wilkie's success was largely due to his ability to combine the treatment of subjects from 'ordinary' life with a standard of craftsmanship that was adjudged by his contemporaries as worthy of comparison with the Dutch masters. Perhaps his most popular work (and indeed probably the most popular painting ever exhibited at the Academy) was *Chelsea Pensioners receiving the*

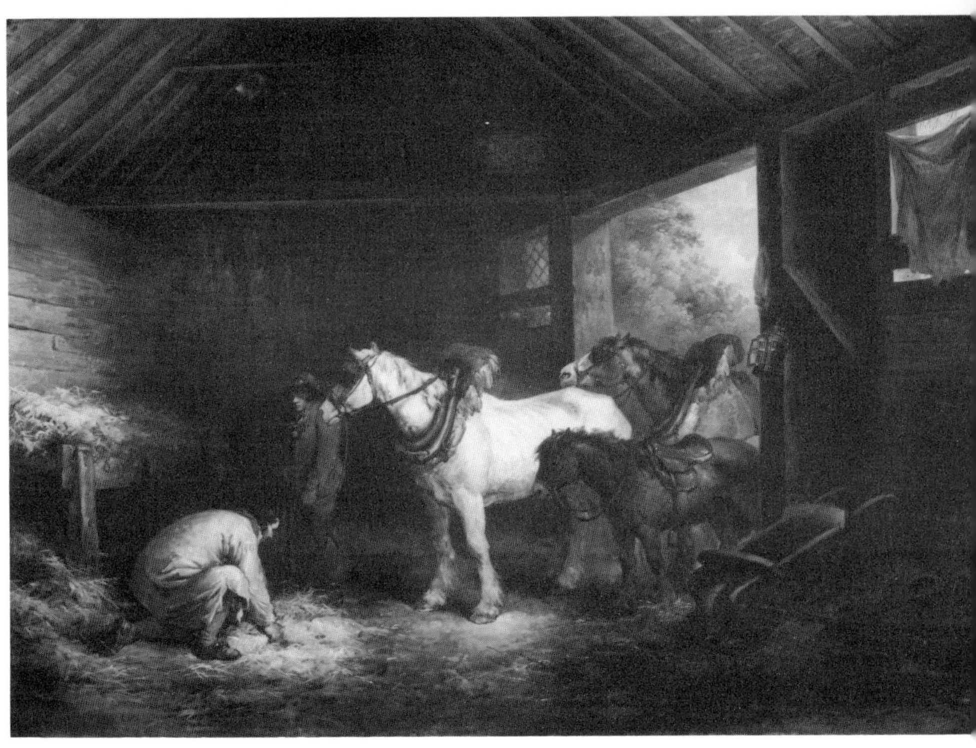

53
GEORGE MORLAND
Inside of a Stable, R.A. 1791
oil on canvas, 148.5 × 203.8cm.(58½ × 80¼in.)
Tate Gallery, London

Gazette announcing the Battle of Waterloo (R.A. 1822, Ill. 55). Its success was such that a protective rail had to be erected in front of it and one newspaper (no doubt conversant with the military techniques used at Waterloo) commented

> The occupation of stations by the hour, in front of favourable pieces, is hardly fair in an exhibition crowded with visitors; and especially when ladies get their poke-bonnets within the frames. The pictures are endangered and all vista shut out. We recommend that on future occasions the pictures of Wilkie may be hung near the ground, there will then be a chance of seeing them. Let the first rank kneel, the second stoop, and the third will only have to cast their eyes down.

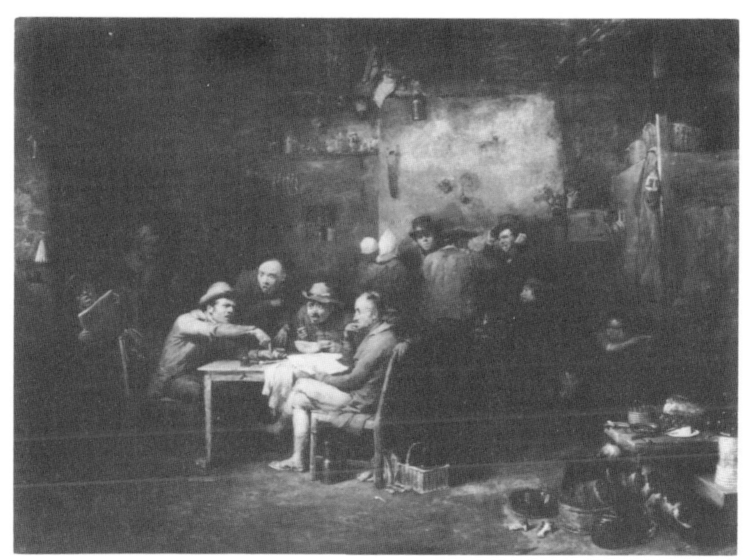

54
SIR DAVID WILKIE, R.A.
The Village Politicians, R.A. 1806
oil on canvas, 57.1 × 74.9cm (22½ × 29½in.)
Private Collection, U.K.

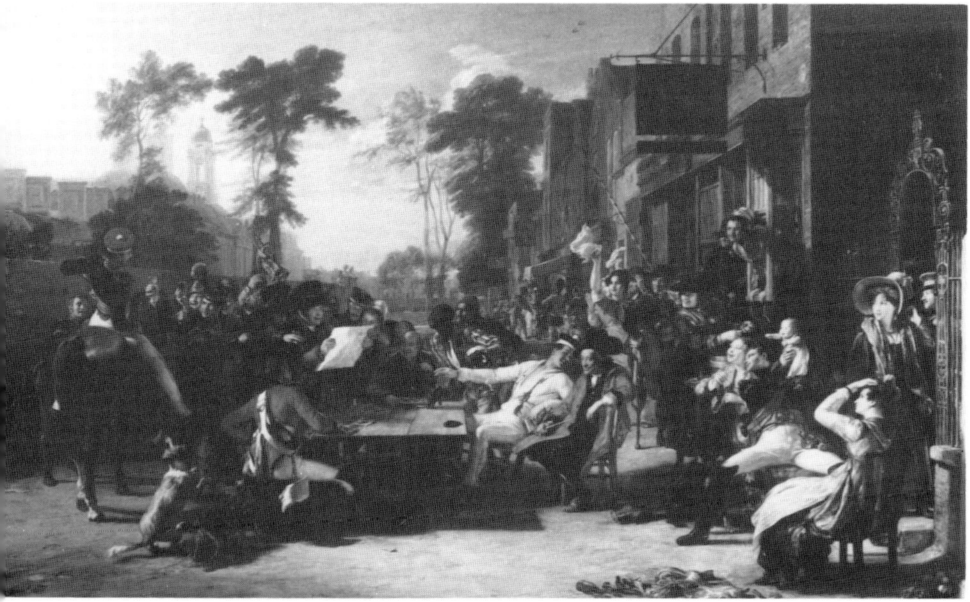

55
SIR DAVID WILKIE, R.A.
Chelsea Pensioners receiving the Gazette announcing the Battle of Waterloo, R.A. 1822
oil on canvas, 101.6 × 157.4cm.(40 × 62in.)
Wellington Museum, Apsley House, London

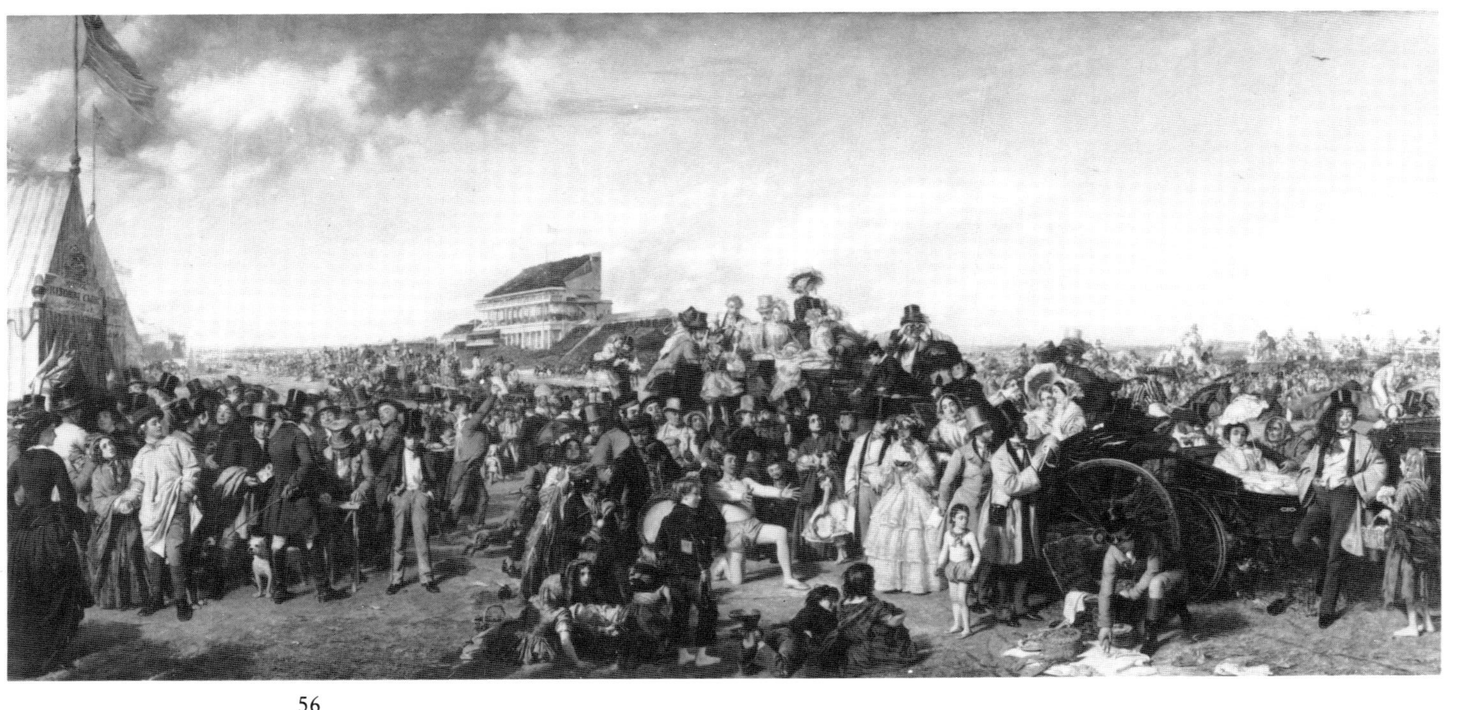

56

WILLIAM POWELL FRITH, R.A.
Derby Day, R.A. 1858
oil on canvas, 101.6 × 223.6cm.(40 × 88in.)
Tate Gallery, London

The picture's popularity is a fair indication of how fast the taste for the sentimental and cloying was growing. Wilkie's true heir was William Powell Frith, whose *Derby Day* (R.A.1858,Ill.56) was the first painting since Wilkie's *Chelsea Pensioners* to have a protective rail placed in front of it (Frith proudly recorded in his autobiography that he was accorded the 'honour' of a rail six times in his career). *Derby Day* is a picture that presented the Victorian public with an attractive but distorted reflection of itself. The work is a series of anecdotes – the country bumpkin, in a smock, being pulled away from a cardsharp on the left; a boy who has lost all his money to the cardsharp; on the right a rake who has married for money (alas! his poor wife); and gypsies, acrobats and the 'contented poor'. It is an amalgam, in short, of posed 'realism' and bogus sentiment, all exquisitely painted but, for all its verisimilitude, bearing little relationship to the truth about England in the 1850s. It is this cultural dishonesty that robs the work of any validity today - and within a decade painters such as Manet and Degas were to fix the reality of their time with a far greater commitment to the truth. *Derby Day* was the second of Frith's 'real-life' panoramas and he followed it with several more, all of them equally devoid of any air in their lungs. In the 1870s however, some awareness of social reality did emerge at the Academy in the works of Luke Fildes, Hubert von Herkomer and Frank Holl, all of whom were to become Academicians. Their early illustrations for the *Graphic* magazine made a deep and lasting impression on Van Gogh. Fildes' *Applicants for Admission to a Casual Ward* (R.A. 1874, Ill. 57) touched a raw nerve in Victorian society. People flocked to see it (doubtless thinking 'there but for the grace ...') but critical reaction was predictable. As the *Art Journal* commented

> there is little in a theme of such grovelling misery to recommend it to a painter whose purpose is beauty... the state of things he represents to us ... is rather a matter for regret.

Fildes' commitment to such themes was to prove sporadic and he eventually became a wealthy and famous Society artist. Herkomer's career developed in a similar manner, an early concern for reality (Ill. 58) eventually disappearing as he became rich and successful. Holl's sympathies remained constant but his comparatively early death prevented him from developing them.

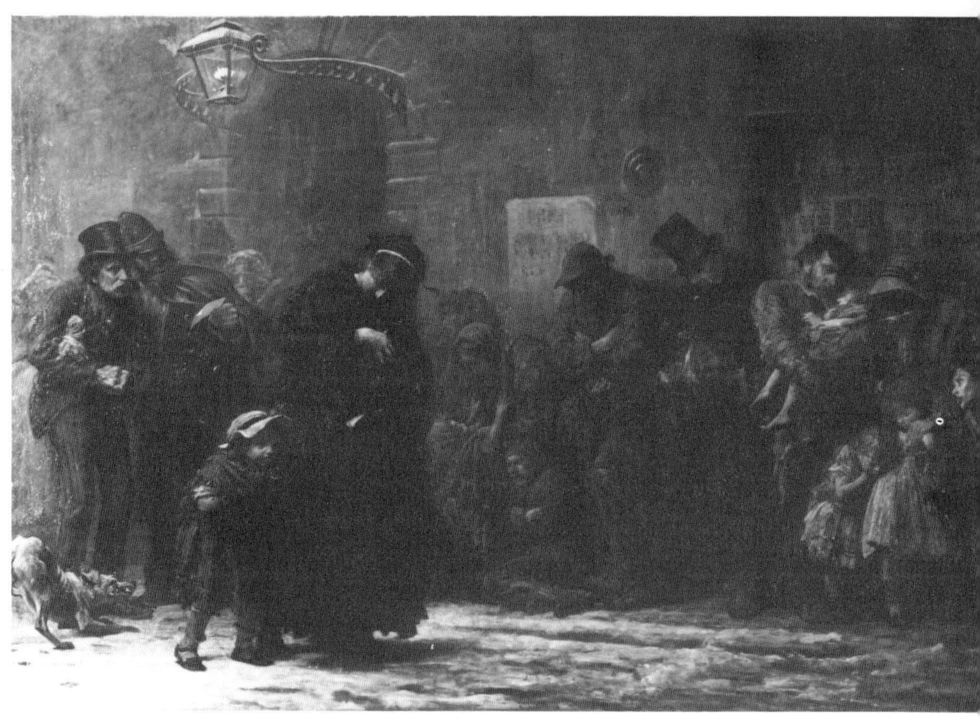

57
SIR LUKE FILDES, R.A.
Applicants for Admission to a Casual Ward
(detail), R.A. 1874
oil on canvas, 142.2 × 242.6cm.(56 × 97½in.)
Royal Holloway College, Egham, Surrey, U.K.

During the twentieth-century the vast growth in the number of independent dealers' galleries has reflected a widespread preference among artists for exhibiting outside large institutions such as the Royal Academy. This has been part of a general reaction throughout Europe against the values of official academies of art since the late nineteenth-century. However, the Royal Academy had exhibited the work of some leading artists during this period (including Sargent, Sickert, Spencer and Lowry) and if during the heyday of Modernism the Academy was restricted in its outlook, the final exhaustion of the Modernist aesthetic has led, paradoxically, to the start of the Academy's revival as a forum for contemporary taste, the readiness of the institution to display a wider range of styles matching the diversity and artistic egalitarianism of post-Modernism itself. In addition, the Academy has evolved a dynamic loan exhibition

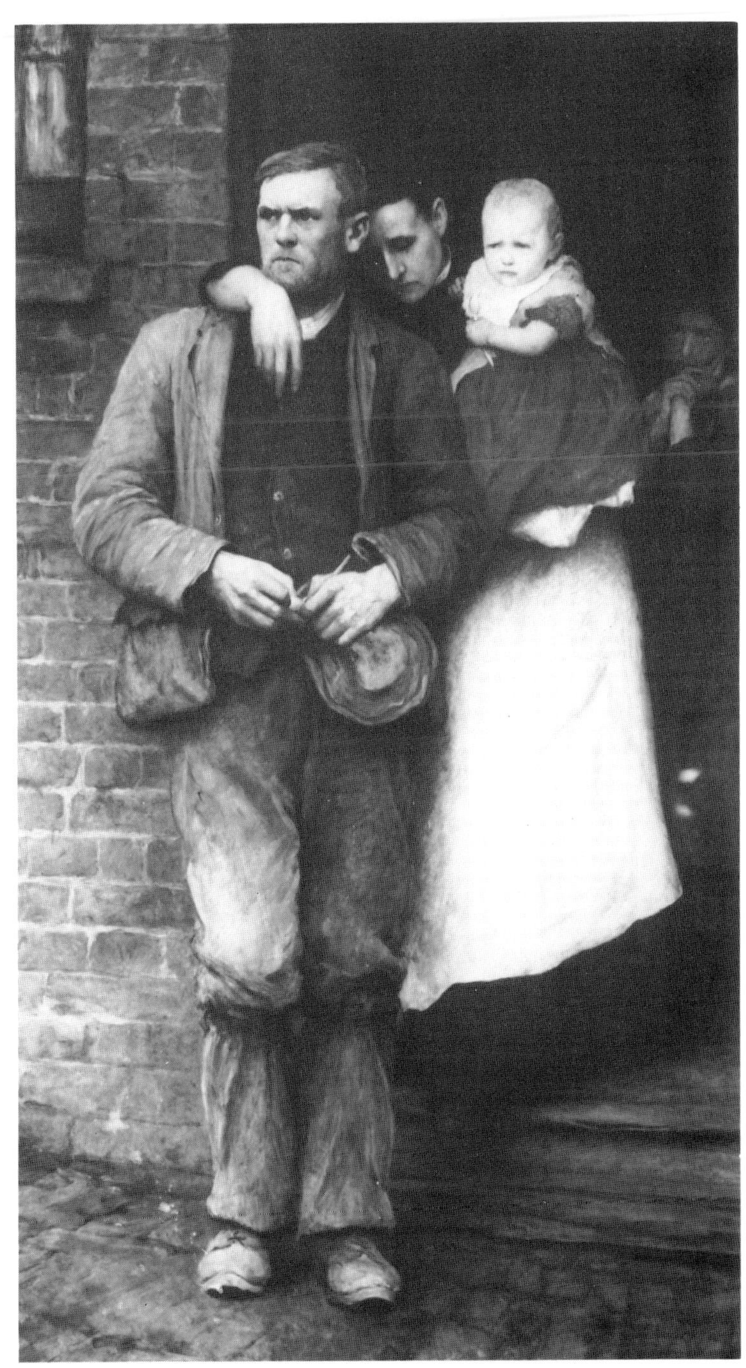

58
HUBERT VON HERKOMER, R.A.
On Strike, R.A. 1891, (Diploma Work)
oil on canvas, 227.9 × 126.3cm.(89¾ × 49¾in.)
Royal Academy of Arts, London

policy (separate from the Summer Exhibition) and can claim, in this respect, to be the leading showplace for art in London today. A great number of recent exhibitions, such as the *Bonnard* of 1967, the *Chinese art* of 1974, the *Turner* bi-centenary of 1974-5 and *Post-Impressionist* show of 1979, as well as the great many smaller exhibitions devoted to contemporary art, all testify to this. The Royal Academy therefore approaches the twenty-first century as an institution that embodies the values of the past and welcomes the challenge of the future.

The Royal Academy is now just over two hundred years old. In that time it has witnessed the arrival and departure of a great number of schools, movements and styles, reflecting every aspect of British life. If in its first century Reynolds' high ideals for historical painting gradually became generally diluted with what he warned against as 'A provision of endless apparatus, a bustle of infinite enquiry and research .. to evade and shuffle off real labour, – the real labour of thinking,' it is true that by 1869 the original aim of the Academy to foster the visual arts had already been largely fulfilled. During that century the institution had signally encouraged the visual arts in Britain, public interest had grown immensely and some of the greatest visual contributions to the culture of the period had been made. When the Academy was founded the public for contemporary art had consisted of a small group of connoisseurs. Few people outside that elite ever had the chance to see, let alone purchase, works of art. A hundred years later the situation had been transformed. By 1869, several national collections were in existence and thriving, the principal patronage of living art had moved away from a declining aristocracy to a growing middle-class and public appreciation of the arts was at its height. Furthermore, Reynolds' serious aspirations for a national school of painting had indeed become a reality comparatively quickly. During that period British art attained the world stage for the first time, and in the works of Turner and Constable, at least, it had achieved an equality with the very greatest art of the past. The Royal Academy, by stimulating the arts through education and exhibition, contributed decisively towards creating that achievement.

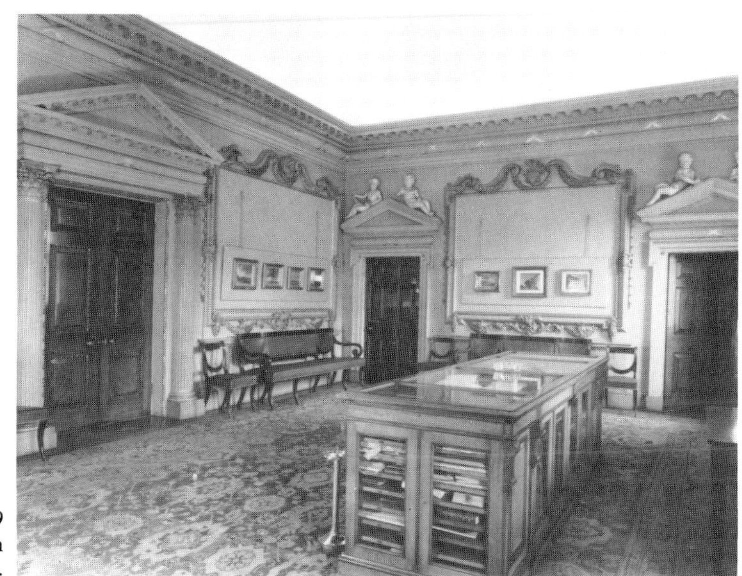

59
The Saloon at Burlington House (photograph).

The Royal Academy and its Possessions

Burlington House was substantially altered and enlarged when the Royal Academy moved into it in the 1850s. The first floor of the old part of Burlington House contains five principal rooms, including the Saloon with a superb ceiling by William Kent, the finest and least altered room from Lord Burlington's time (Ill. 59). Another of the five rooms is the Council Room which contains the original ceiling paintings by Sebastiano Ricci. Another work by him adorns the ceiling of the General Assembly Room. The ballroom of the old house is now the Reynolds Room which adjoins the Council Room. The entrance hall contains pictures by Angelica Kauffman and Benjamin West which were removed from the Fine Rooms at Somerset House for which they were painted. The imposing staircase is surmounted by William

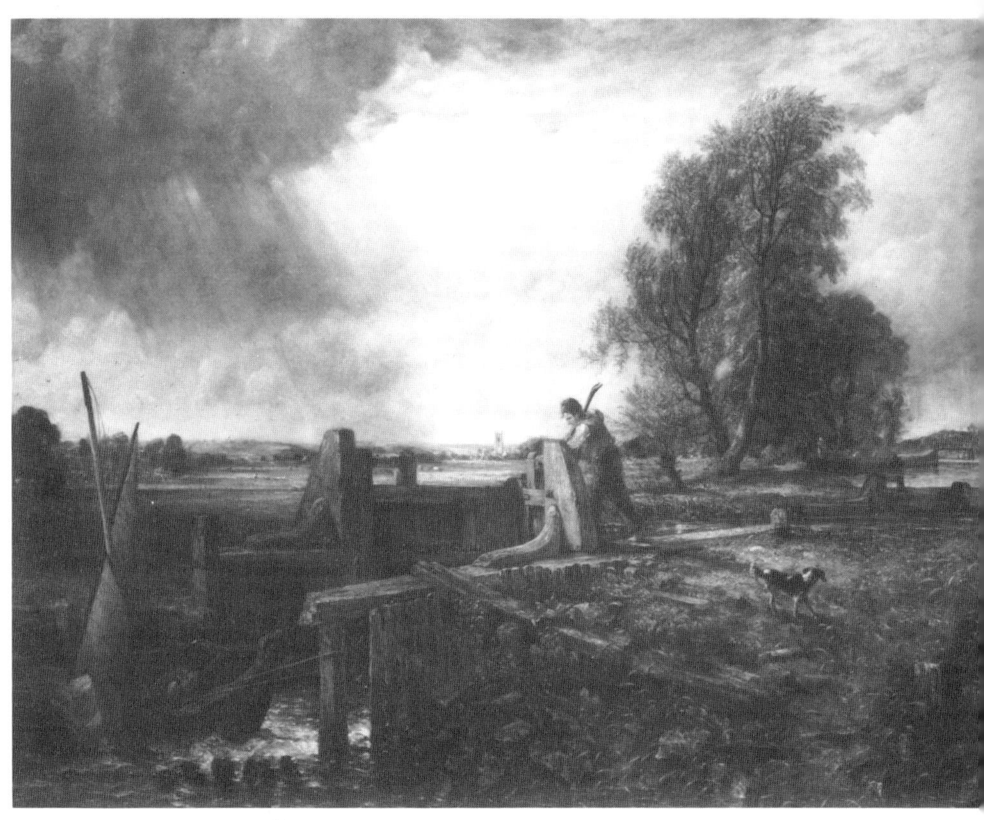

60
JOHN CONSTABLE, R.A.
A Boat passing a Lock, 1826
Diploma Work, exhibited R.A. 1829
oil on canvas, 101.6 × 127cm.(40 × 50in.)
Royal Academy of Arts, London

Kent's roundel of *Architecture contemplating the portrait of Inigo Jones* and on either side are decorations by Sebastiano Ricci which were also retained from the original Burlington House. In niches at the top of the stairs are statues of Gainsborough on the left and Turner on the right.

Over the years the Academy has built up an impressive collection of works of art, including all the Diploma works. These include several masterpieces such as Turner's *Dolbadern Castle, North Wales,* Constable's *Boat Passing a Lock* (Ill. 60), E.W. Cooke's *Scheveningen Pinks off Yarmouth,* Fuseli's *Thor and the serpent of Midgard* and Herkomer's *On Strike* (Ill. 58). The Diploma collection also includes excellent pictures by Reynolds,

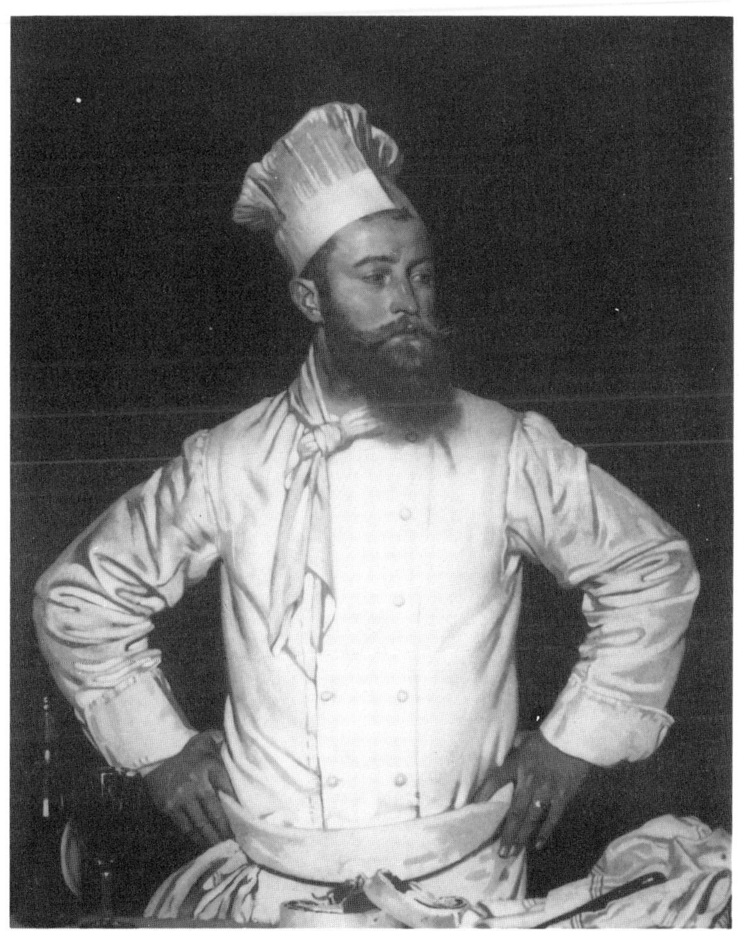

61
SIR WILLIAM ORPEN, R.A.
Le Chef de l'Hotel Chatham, Paris, 1919
Diploma Work, exhibited R.A. 1921
oil on canvas, 124.4 × 101.6cm.(49 × 40in.)
Royal Academy of Arts, London

Wilson, Raeburn, David Roberts, John Frederick Lewis, Edwin Landseer, Augustus Wall Callcott and Sir William Orpen (Ill.61).

The Academy also owns other fine objects: portraits by Reynolds and Gainsborough; fifteen sketches by Constable, a gift from his daughter; his painting *The Leaping Horse;* a number of drawings made by Stubbs for *The Anatomy of the Horse;* fifty-three profile drawings of Academy members made by George Dance; and Turner's portable watercolour box.

Perhaps the greatest work owned by the Academy, however, is the 'Taddei Madonna' by Michelangelo Buonarotti, *The Madonna and Child with the Infant St. John* (Ill. 62). Michelangelo carved this Carrara marble relief in 1504-5, soon after completing the *David*. Its first owner was the Florentine patron, Taddeo Taddei, in whose family the work remained until early in the nineteenth century when it was acquired by a French collector named J.B. Wicar who sold it to Sir George Beaumont for about £1000. It was bequeathed to the Academy by Beaumont's widow in 1830. It is one of the very few Michelangelo sculptures outside Italy, and its ownership would surely have delighted Reynolds; his veneration for the artist led him to say at the end of his final Discourse

> ...I should desire that the last words which I should pronounce in this Academy, and from this place, might be the name of – MICHELANGELO.

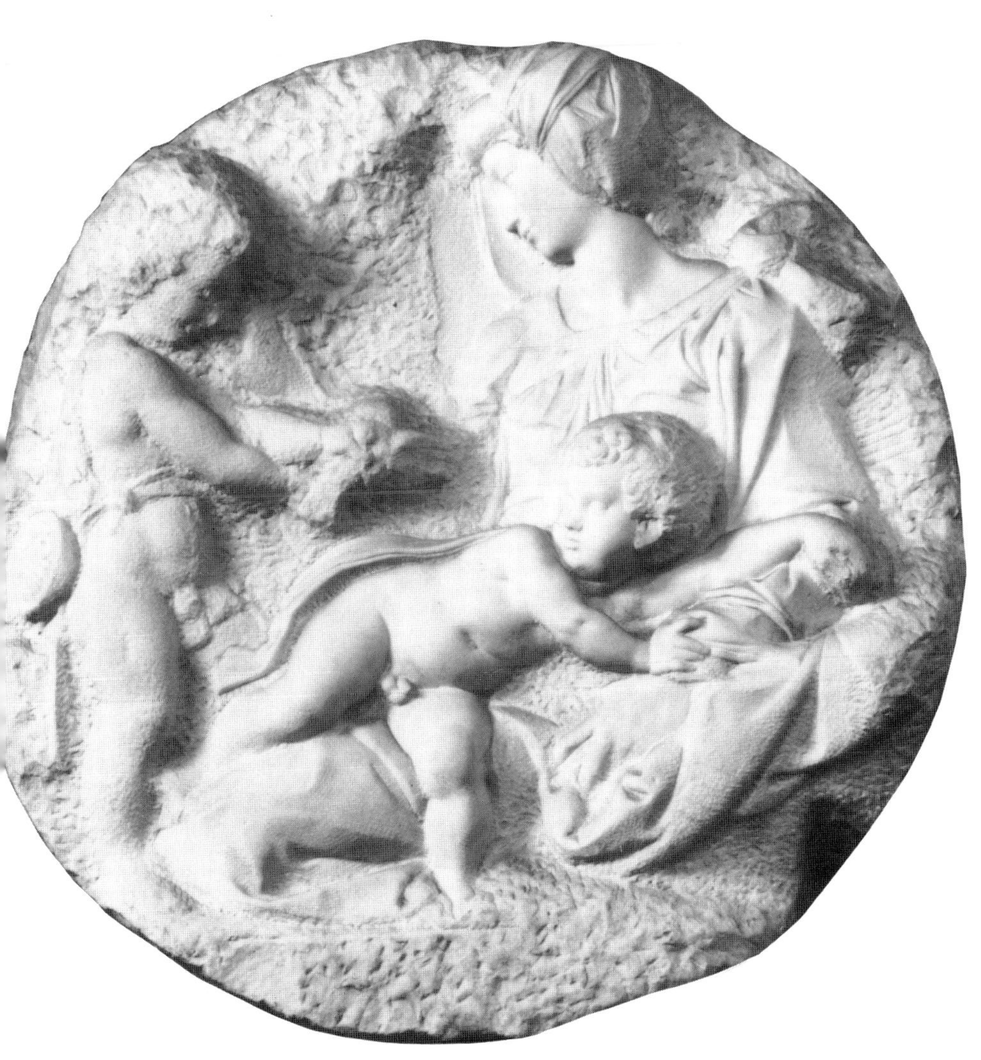

62
MICHELANGELO BUONARROTI
Madonna and Child with the Infant St. John, 1504-5,
Carrara marble relief
diameter 109.2cm.(43in.)
Royal Academy of Arts, London

Acknowledgements

The author wishes to thank the staff of the Royal Academy for their assistance, and in particular Sidney C Hutchison. His book, *The History of the Royal Academy* is the authoritative account of the development and progress of the institution and it has been of inestimable value. Others to be thanked are Hazell Elliott; Hans Fletcher; Constance Anne Parker; Marie Basalmidi; and Shaun Morgan.

E.S